STEP Ladder

STEP 3

(900-word Level)

シャーロック・ホームズの冒険

「赤毛組合」「まだらの紐」

Adventures of Sherlock Holmes

Sir Arthur Conan Doyle

コナン・ドイル

はじめに

みなさんは英語で何ができるようになりたいですか。

外国人と自由にコミュニケーションしたい
インターネット上の英語のサイトや、ペーパーバック、英字新聞を辞書なしで読めるようになりたい
字幕なしで洋画を見たい
受験や就職で有利になりたい
海外で活躍したい……

英語の基礎的な力、とりわけ読解力をつけるのに大切なのは、楽しみながら多読することです。数多くの英文に触れることによって、英語の発想や表現になじみ、英語の力が自然に身についてきます。

そうは言っても、何から手をつけていいのかわからないということはないでしょうか。やさしそうだと思って、外国の絵本や子ども向けの洋書を買ってはみたものの、知らない単語や表現ばかりが出てきて、途中で読むのをあきらめた経験がある方もいらっしゃるのではありませんか。

おすすめしたいのは、学習者向けにやさしく書かれた本から始めて、自分のレベルに合わせて、少しずつ難しいものに移っていく読み方です。

本書《ステップラダー・シリーズ》は、使用する単語を限定した、やさしい英語で書かれている英文リーダーで、初心者レベルの方でも、無理なく最後まで読めるように工夫されています。

みなさんが、楽しみながら英語の力をステップアップできるようになっています。

特長と使い方

●特長●

ステップラダー・シリーズは、世界の古典や名作などを、使用する単語を限定して、やさしい表現に書き改めた、英語初級〜初中級者向けの英文リーダーです。見開きごとのあらすじや、すべての単語の意味が載ったワードリストなど、初心者レベルでも負担なく、英文が読めるように構成されています。無料音声ダウンロード付きですので、文字と音声の両面で読書を楽しむことができます。

ステップ	使用語彙数	対象レベル	英検	CEFR
STEP 1	300語	中学1年生程度	5級	A1
STEP 2	600語	中学2年生程度	4級	A1
STEP 3	900語	中学3年生程度	3級	A2

●使い方●

- 本文以外のパートはすべてヘルプです。できるだけ本文に集中して読みましょう。
- 日本語の語順に訳して読むと速く読むことができません。文の頭から順番に、意味のかたまりごとに理解するようにしましょう。
- すべてを100パーセント理解しようとせず、ところどころ想像で補うようにして、ストーリーに集中する方が、楽に楽しく読めます。
- 黙読する、音読する、音声に合わせて読む、音声だけを聞くなど、いろいろな読み方をしてみましょう。

●無料音声ダウンロード●

本書の朗読音声（MP3形式）を、下記URLとQRコードから無料でダウンロードすることができます。

www.ibcpub.co.jp/step_ladder/0662/

※PCや端末、ソフトウェアの操作・再生方法については、編集部ではお答えできません。製造元にお問い合わせいただくか、インターネットで検索するなどして解決してください。

●構成●

語数表示
開いたページの単語数と、読んできた総単語数が確認できます。

トラック番号
朗読音声の番号です。

The Red-Headed League 3

01 One day last fall, I visited my friend, Mr. Sherlock Holmes. He was deep in conversation with a short, heavy, older man who had red hair.

[1]"Ah, you have come at a perfect time, my dear Watson," Holmes said with a smile.

"But you are busy," I said. "I am sorry to interrupt."

"Not at all. Mr. Wilson, this is my friend, Mr. Watson. He helps me in all my work. I think he will help me on your case, too."

We shook hands and I sat down to join the two men.

[2]"I know that you are interested in my cases, because you have written so many of them into stories," said my friend.

私が友人のシャーロック・ホームズを訪ねると、彼は赤髪の年輩男と話していた。「いい時に来たね、親愛なるワトソン」とホームズは笑顔で言った。

"Your cases have always been interesting to me, it is true," I said.

(128 [128] words)

✤ KEYWORDS

- □ **red-headed** [rédhédıd]
- □ **league** [lí:g]
- □ **Sherlock Holmes** [ʃə́:ʳlɑ̀:k hóumz]
- □ **conversation** [kɑ̀:nvəʳséıʃən]
- □ **Watson** [wɑ́:tsən]
- □ **interrupt** [ìntərʌ́pt]
- □ **Wilson** [wílsən]
- □ **case** [kéıs]
- □ *shake hands*

✤ KEY SENTENCES (☞ p. 84)

[1] "Ah, • you have come • at a perfect time, • my dear Watson," • Holmes said • with a smile.

[2] "I know that • you are interested in my cases, • because you have written • so many of them • into stories," • said my friend.

あらすじ
本文のおおまかな内容がわかります。

キーセンテンス
長い文や難しい表現の文を、意味単位に区切って紹介しています。表示のページに訳があります。

キーワード
使用語彙以外で使われている初出の単語、熟語のリストです。発音記号の読み方は次ページの表を参考にしてください。

キーワードについて

1. 語尾が規則変化する単語は原形、不規則変化語は本文で出てきた形を見出しにしています。

例 studies/studying/studied → study
goes/going → go
went → went
gone → gone

2. 熟語に含まれる所有格の人称代名詞(my, your, his/her, theirなど)は one's に、再帰代名詞(myself, yourselfなど)は oneself に置き換えています。

例 do your best → do one's best
enjoy myself → enjoy oneself

3. 熟語に含まれるbe動詞 (is, are, was, were)は原形のbeに置き換えています。

例 was going to → be going to

発音記号表 

●母音●

/ɑ/	**h**o**t**, **l**o**t**
/ɑː/	**ar**m, **ar**t, c**ar**, h**ar**d, m**ar**ch, p**ar**k, f**a**ther
/æ/	**a**sk, b**a**g, c**a**t, d**a**nce, h**a**nd, m**a**n, th**a**nk
/aɪ/	**i**ce, n**i**ce, r**i**ce, t**i**me, wh**i**te, b**uy**, **eye**, fl**y**
/aɪə^r/	f**ire**, t**ire**
/aʊ/	br**ow**n, d**ow**n, n**ow**, h**ou**se, m**ou**th, **ou**t
/aʊə^r/	fl**ower**, sh**ower**, t**ower**, h**our**
/e/	b**e**d, **e**gg, fri**e**nd, h**ea**d, h**e**lp, l**e**tter, p**e**t, r**e**d
/eɪ/	c**a**ke, m**a**ke, f**a**ce, g**a**me, n**a**me, d**ay**, pl**ay**
/eə^r/	c**are**, ch**air**, h**air**
/ɪ/	b**i**g, f**i**sh, g**i**ve, l**i**sten, m**i**lk, p**i**nk, s**i**ng
/iː/	**ea**t, r**ea**d, sp**ea**k, gr**ee**n, m**ee**t, w**ee**k, p**eo**ple
/ɪə^r/	d**ear**, **ear**, n**ear**, y**ear**
/oʊ/	c**o**ld, g**o**, h**o**me, n**o**te, **o**ld, c**oa**t, kn**ow**
/ɔː/	**a**ll, b**a**ll, c**a**ll, t**a**lk, w**a**lk
/ɔː^r/	d**oor**, m**ore**, sh**or**t
/ɔɪ/	b**oy**, enj**oy**, t**oy**
/ʊ/	b**oo**k, c**oo**k, f**oo**t, g**oo**d, l**oo**k, p**u**t
/uː/	f**oo**d, r**oo**m, sch**oo**l, fr**ui**t, j**ui**ce
/ʊə^r/	p**ure**, s**ure**
/əː^r/	b**ir**d, g**ir**l, th**ir**d, l**ear**n, t**ur**n, w**or**k
/ʌ/	b**u**s, cl**u**b, j**u**mp, l**u**nch, r**u**n, l**o**ve, m**o**ther
/ə/	**a**bout, **o**'clock
/i/	eas**y**, mon**ey**, ver**y**

●子音●

/b/	**b**ag, **b**all, **b**ed, **b**ig, **b**ook, clu**b**, jo**b**
/d/	**d**esk, **d**og, **d**oor, col**d**, foo**d**, frien**d**
/f/	**f**ace, **f**inger, **f**ish, **f**ood, hal**f**, i**f**, lau**gh**
/g/	**g**ame, **g**irl, **g**o, **g**ood, bi**g**, do**g**, e**gg**
/h/	**h**air, **h**and, **h**appy, **h**ome, **h**ot
/j/	**y**ellow, **y**es, **y**oung
/k/	**c**ake, **c**oo**k**, **k**ing, des**k**, loo**k**, mil**k**, pin**k**, tal**k**
/l/	**l**earn, **l**eg, **l**itt**l**e, **l**ook, anima**l**, gir**l**, schoo**l**
/m/	**m**ake, **m**other, **m**ovie, ho**m**e, na**m**e, roo**m**, ti**m**e
/n/	k**n**ow, **n**ame, **n**ight, **n**oo**n**, pe**n**, ru**n**, trai**n**
/p/	**p**ark, **p**encil, **p**et, **p**ink, ca**p**, hel**p**, jum**p**, sto**p**
/r/	**r**ead, **r**ed, **r**ice, **r**oom, **r**un, w**r**ite
/s/	**s**ay, **s**ee, **s**ong, **s**tudy, **s**ummer, bu**s**, fa**c**e, i**c**e
/t/	**t**alk, **t**eacher, **t**ime, **t**rain, ca**t**, foo**t**, ha**t**, nigh**t**
/v/	**v**ery, **v**ideo, **v**isit, fi**v**e, gi**v**e, ha**v**e, lo**v**e, mo**v**ie
/w/	**w**alk, **w**ant, **w**eek, **w**oman, **w**ork
/z/	**z**ero, **z**oo, clothe**s**, ha**s**, mu**s**ic, no**s**e
/ʃ/	**sh**ip, **sh**ort, Engli**sh**, fi**sh**, sta**ti**on
/ʒ/	mea**s**ure, lei**s**ure, televi**s**ion
/ŋ/	ki**ng**, lo**ng**, si**ng**, spri**ng**, E**ng**lish, dri**n**k, tha**n**k
/tʃ/	**ch**air, **ch**eap, ca**tch**, lun**ch**, mar**ch**, tea**ch**er, wa**tch**
/θ/	**th**ank, **th**ink, **th**ursday, bir**th**day, mon**th**, mou**th**, too**th**
/ð/	**th**ey, **th**is, **th**en, ba**th**e, bro**th**er, fa**th**er, mo**th**er
/dʒ/	**J**apan, **j**ump, **j**unior, bri**dg**e, chan**g**e, en**j**oy, oran**g**e

Contents

●「赤毛組合」に登場する主な人物

Jabez Wilson　ジェイベズ・ウィルソン　燃えるような赤髪の初老の男性で小さな質屋の店主。

Vincent Spaulding　ヴィンセント・スポールディング　ウィルソンの店で働いている。

Duncan Ross　ダンカン・ロス　赤毛組合の事務所でウィルソンを審査する。

●「まだらの紐」に登場する主な人物

Helen Stoner　ヘレン・ストーナー　事件の依頼人。朝早くにホームズの部屋に来る。

sister　ヘレンの姉　２年前に「まだらの紐」という言葉を遺し、不可解な死を遂げる。

Dr. Roylott　ロイロット博士　ストーナー姉妹の義父。医師だが気性が激しい。

【ホームズのトレードマーク】

「シャーロック・ホームズ」といえば、パイプを片手に鹿撃ち帽をかぶり、ケープ付きのコートを身にまとった姿をイメージされる方も多いでしょう。

・ホームズが映画などでいつも咥えている吸い口が大きく曲がったパイプは「キャラバッシュ・パイプ」。

・「鹿撃ち帽」は、19世紀後半に英国で狩猟用に使われた帽子で、前後に庇（ひさし）、側面に頭の上で結んで留められるようになった耳当てがついています。

・丈の長いコートの外側に肩全体を覆うケープが付いた「インバネス・コート」は、スコットランドのインバネス地方で、屋外でバグパイプを雨風から守って演奏するために作られたものと言われています。

しかし、これらのアイテムは原作中には描写がなく、挿絵や演劇などによって二次的に生み出されものです。鹿撃ち帽は「ボスコム渓谷の惨劇」でシドニー・パジェットが描いた挿絵のイメージが原点と考えられています。そして現在まで広く浸透している、パイプ、帽子、コートの3点が揃ったホームズ像は、米国の俳優ウィリアム・ジレットが、舞台でホームズを演じる際に脚色し形作ったものです。

The Red-Headed League

赤毛組合

One day last fall, I visited my friend, Mr. Sherlock Holmes. He was deep in conversation with a short, heavy, older man who had red hair.

[1]"Ah, you have come at a perfect time, my dear Watson," Holmes said with a smile.

"But you are busy," I said. "I am sorry to interrupt."

"Not at all. Mr. Wilson, this is my friend, Mr. Watson. He helps me in all my work. I think he will help me on your case, too."

We shook hands and I sat down to join the two men.

[2]"I know that you are interested in my cases, because you have written so many of them into stories," said my friend.

私が友人のシャーロック・ホームズを訪ねると、彼は赤髪の年輩男と話していた。「いい時に来たね、親愛なるワトソン」とホームズは笑顔で言った。

"Your cases have always been interesting to me, it is true," I said.

(128 [128] words)

✤ KEYWORDS

- ☐ **red-headed** [rédhédɪd]
- ☐ **league** [líːg]
- ☐ **Sherlock Holmes** [ʃə́ːʳlɑ̀ːk hóʊmz]
- ☐ **conversation** [kɑ̀ːnvəʳséɪʃən]
- ☐ **Watson** [wɑ́ːtsən]
- ☐ **interrupt** [ìntərʌ́pt]
- ☐ **Wilson** [wílsən]
- ☐ **case** [kéɪs]
- ☐ *shake hands*

✤ KEY SENTENCES (☞ p. 84)

1 "Ah, • you have come • at a perfect time, • my dear Watson," • Holmes said • with a smile.

2 "I know • that you are interested in my cases, • because you have written • so many of them • into stories," • said my friend.

“You say you are interested in these cases because they are so different from normal, everyday life,” Holmes said. “But I often tell you that the strangest things happen in the smallest crimes.”

“And I still don’t believe you,” I said.

[3]“Well, I think we have a case that will finally make you see things my way,” said my friend with a smile. He turned to the older man.

“Mr. Wilson, please begin your story again,” Holmes said. “Please do this not just for Mr. Watson, but for myself as well. Your story is so unusual that I would like to hear all the details again. [4]Usually, when I study a case, I think of thousands of other cases like it. But in this case, I cannot think of a single similar one. Your story is very unique.”

ホームズは赤髪の男ウィルソンに、その珍しい話をもう一度詳しく話すように頼んだ。彼はポケットから新聞を取り出すと広告のページを見せた。

The heavy man pulled a piece of newspaper from his pocket. He showed us the advertisement page.

(155 [283] words)

✤ KEYWORDS

- ☐ **normal** [nɔ́:ʳməl]
- ☐ **everyday** [évridéɪ]
- ☐ **crime** [kráɪm]
- ☐ *as well*
- ☐ **unusual** [ənjúːʒwəl]
- ☐ **detail** [dɪtéɪl]
- ☐ *think of*
- ☐ **single** [síŋgəl]
- ☐ **unique** [juːníːk]
- ☐ **newspaper** [núːzpèɪpəʳ]
- ☐ **advertisement** [æ̀dvəʳtáɪzmənt]

✤ KEY SENTENCES (☞ p. 84)

3 "Well, • I think we have a case • that will finally • make you see things • my way," • said my friend • with a smile.

4 Usually, • when I study a case, • I think of • thousands of other cases • like it.

The man looked like a normal laborer. His clothes were old. The only unusual thing about him was his hair, which was as red as fire.

Sherlock Holmes was watching me. He smiled and said, “I can tell that Mr. Wilson has been a laborer. [5]He believes in God, he has been to China, and recently he has done a lot of writing.”

Mr. Wilson was surprised to hear Holmes say all this.

“How do you know all that about me?”

“Well,” Holmes began, “the muscles of your right hand are larger. So you have worked hard with it. The little cross you wear on your coat shows you are religious. [6]The bottom of your right sleeve is shiny because you have moved it along your writing paper as you sat at a desk writing, while the left elbow is thin where you rested it on the desk.”

(148 [431] words)

ウィルソンは普通の労働者に見えるが、髪の色が火のように赤かった。自分のことをいろいろ言い当てられて驚く彼に、ホームズは種明かしをした。

✤ KEYWORDS

- ☐ **laborer** [léɪbəʳer]
- ☐ **god** [gɑ́:d]
- ☐ **China** [tʃáɪnə]
- ☐ **recently** [rí:səntli]
- ☐ **muscle** [mʌ́səl]
- ☐ **cross** [krɔ́:s]
- ☐ **religious** [rɪlídʒəs]
- ☐ **bottom** [bɑ́:təm]
- ☐ **sleeve** [slí:v]
- ☐ **shiny** [ʃáɪni]
- ☐ *writing paper*
- ☐ **elbow** [élbòʊ]
- ☐ **thin** [θín]

✤ KEY SENTENCES (☞ p. 84)

5 He believes in God, • he has been to China, • and recently • he has done a lot of writing.

6 The bottom of your right sleeve is shiny • because you have moved it • along your writing paper • as you sat at a desk • writing, • while the left elbow is thin • where you rested it • on the desk.

"What about China?"

"[7]I see a tattoo on your hand which could only have been painted in China. That light pink color only comes out of China. I also see a coin from China on your watch chain. It was all very simple."

Mr. Wilson laughed loudly. "Well, at first I thought there was some magic, but I see it is very simple."

"Maybe I should not tell all my secrets, Watson. [8]No one will be impressed with me any more if I tell everything. Please show us your advertisement, Mr. Wilson."

"Here," he said. "Read it for yourself."

Holmes took the paper and began to read:

ホームズは新聞の広告を読み上げた。「赤毛の男を募集。20歳以上の健常者。簡単な仕事。週給４ポンド。月曜11時に事務所に直接申し込むこと」

"Opening for one red-headed man. Must be healthy and strong, over twenty years old. Easy work. Pay: four pounds a week. Apply in person on Monday, at eleven o'clock, at the office of the League, Fleet Street."

(144 [575] words)

✤ KEYWORDS

- ☐ **tattoo** [tæ̀túː]
- ☐ *come out of*
- ☐ **magic** [mǽdʒɪk]
- ☐ **secret** [síːkrət]
- ☐ **impressed** [ìmprést]
- ☐ **opening** [óʊp(ə)nɪŋ]
- ☐ **healthy** [hélθi]
- ☐ **pay** [péɪ]
- ☐ **pound** [páʊnd]
- ☐ **apply** [əpláɪ]
- ☐ *in person*
- ☐ **Fleet Street** [flíːt stríːt]

✤ KEY SENTENCES (☞ p. 84)

7 I see a tattoo • on your hand • which could only have been painted • in China.

8 No one will be impressed with me • any more • if I tell everything.

“What does it mean?” I asked.

Holmes laughed. “It is unusual, isn’t it? Now, Mr. Wilson, tell us how this advertisement has affected your life. Note the date of the paper, Watson.”

“April 27, 1890. Just two months ago.”

“Very good. Now, Mr. Wilson?”

“Well, I have a small pawnshop in London, but I do not make much money there. I can only have one helper, and he comes for only half pay to learn the business.”

“His name?”

“Vincent Spaulding. [9]I know he could make better money doing something else, but if he wants to work for me, I will not stop him.”

新聞の日付は２か月前。ウィルソンは小さな質屋を営んでいて、ヴィンセント・スポールディングという通常の給料の半額で働く助手を雇っていた。

"You are lucky to get someone to work for you at less than the normal pay. [10]I think he may be as unusual as the advertisement you have read us."

(134 [709] words)

✤ KEYWORDS

- ☐ **affect** [əfékt]
- ☐ **note** [nóʊt]
- ☐ **pawnshop** [pɔ́:nʃɑ̀:p]
- ☐ **London** [lʌ́ndən]
- ☐ **helper** [hélpəʳ]
- ☐ *come for*
- ☐ **Vincent Spaulding** [vínsent spɔ́:ldɪŋ]
- ☐ **less** [lés]

✤ KEY SENTENCES (☞ p. 84–85)

[9] I know • he could make better money • doing something else, • but if he wants to work • for me, • I will not stop him.

[10] I think • he may be • as unusual as the advertisement • you have read us.

"Oh, he is all right, but he has his problems. He is always taking pictures. Then he runs downstairs to develop them. But he works hard."

"He is working for you now?"

"Yes, he and a girl of fourteen live with me. She cooks and keeps things clean. I have no other family. We live very quiet lives. It was that advertisement that changed everything. [11]Spaulding brought it to me saying, 'I wish I had red hair, Mr. Wilson.' So I asked him why. He said, 'This job at the League of the Red-headed Men—it is such easy work and so well-paid. They always need more men than they can find.'

"You see, Mr. Holmes, I stay mostly at home. I often spend weeks in my home and office without going outside. But Spaulding kept telling me about this job. So I asked him, 'What kind of a job is it?'

スポールディングはよく働くが、いつも写真を撮っては現像するために階下に走っていくという。広告は彼がウィルソン氏に紹介したものだった。

"'It is very easy and you can continue working here. [12]But you will be paid a couple hundred pounds a year extra.'

(173 [882] words)

✤ KEYWORDS

- ☐ **downstairs** [dáʊnstéəʳz]
- ☐ **develop** [dɪvéləp]
- ☐ *I wish*
- ☐ **well-paid** [wèlpéɪd]
- ☐ **paid** [péɪd] < pay
- ☐ **couple** [kʌ́pəl]
- ☐ **extra** [ékstrə]

✤ KEY SENTENCES (☞ p. 85)

[11]Spaulding brought it • to me • saying, • 'I wish • I had red hair, • Mr. Wilson.'

[12]But you will be paid • a couple hundred pounds • a year extra.

"Then I began to be interested, because the money would be useful.

"'Tell me about it,' I said.

"'The League was founded by an American millionaire who felt sympathy for other red-headed men. He left all his money to a club which has the power to give money to any red-headed man.'

"'But there must be thousands of men asking for the money,' I said.

"'No, because your hair must be blazing like fire. Not light red, or dark red. [13] I am sure that you would get the job if you went to the office next Monday, sir.'

"I decided to try for the job. I asked Spaulding to come with me. He was happy to have a day off work.

赤毛組合は米国の大富豪が赤毛の男性のために設立したものだった。行けばきっと仕事がもらえると言われて、ウィルソンは挑戦する気になった。

"[14]Well, on that Monday at eleven o'clock, every man who had even a little red in his hair had come to the office of the League. There was every color of red: strawberry, orange, liver, brick, Irish-setter. But no one had that blazing color that was mentioned in the advertisement.

(171 [1,053] words)

✤ KEYWORDS

- ☐ **found** [fáʊnd]
- ☐ **American** [əmérɪkən]
- ☐ **millionaire** [mìljənéəʳ]
- ☐ **sympathy** [símpəθi]
- ☐ **blazing** [bléɪzɪŋ]
- ☐ **sir** [sə́ːʳ]
- ☐ *day off work*
- ☐ **strawberry** [strɔ́ːbèri]
- ☐ **liver** [lívəʳ]
- ☐ **brick** [brík]
- ☐ **irish-setter** [áɪrɪʃsétəʳ]
- ☐ **mention** [ménʃən]

✤ KEY SENTENCES (☞ p. 85)

[13]I am sure • that you would get the job • if you went to the office • next Monday, • sir.

[14]Well, • on that Monday • at eleven o'clock, • every man • who had even a little red • in his hair • had come to the office • of the League.

"When I saw all those men, I felt discouraged and wanted to go home. But Spaulding wouldn't let me. He pulled me into the office. We had to push through hundreds of bodies."

"Such an interesting story," Holmes said. "Please continue."

"There was a man behind a desk. His hair was even redder than mine. [15]Every red-headed man who came up to him, he asked a question and then sent him away. It seemed to be very difficult to get this job. However, when Spaulding and I entered, he closed the door behind us so we could talk privately.

"'This is Mr. Jabez Wilson,' said Spaulding. 'He would like to apply for the job.'

"'He is very qualified for the job,' the man said. He stared for a long time at my hair until I felt embarrassed. Then suddenly he jumped up and shook my hand. He congratulated me!

応募者のあまりの多さにウィルソンは帰りたくなるが、スポールディングが許さない。事務所に入ると机の後ろに赤髪の男がいてウィルソンを祝福した。

"'Now, please excuse me. I must check your hair,' he said. He began to pull on my hair very hard. I yelled with pain and he stopped.

(176 [1,229] words)

✤ KEYWORDS

- ☐ **discouraged** [dɪskə́:rɪdʒd]
- ☐ **let** [lét]
- ☐ *push through*
- ☐ *come up to*
- ☐ *send ~ away*
- ☐ **seem** [sí:m]
- ☐ **privately** [práɪvətli]
- ☐ **Jabez** [dʒéɪbez]
- ☐ **qualified** [kwɑ́:ləfàɪd]
- ☐ **stare** [stéəʳ]
- ☐ **embarrassed** [ɪmbérəst]
- ☐ *jump up*
- ☐ **congratulate** [kəngrǽtʃəlèɪt]
- ☐ **yell** [jél]

✤ KEY SENTENCES (☞ p. 85)

15 Every red-headed man • who came up to him, • he asked a question • and then • sent him away.

"'It is real hair. There are tears in your eyes,' he said. [16]Then he opened the door and shouted to the crowd that the job was taken.

"'My name is Duncan Ross,' he told me. 'I am glad to meet you. Do you have a family, Mr. Wilson?'

"I answered that I did not.

"'Dear me!' he said, 'that is very serious! I am sorry to hear that. [17]This money was given to our organization so that more red-headed sons could be born.'

"I was afraid that I did not have the job, then he said: 'However, your hair is so unusually red, that we will let you join anyway. When can you begin?'

"'It is a little difficult,' I said, 'for I have a business already. What are the hours?'

"'Ten to two.'

男はダンカン・ロスと名乗った。仕事は10時から２時まで。ウィルソンは昼間は事務所で働いて、その間質屋はスポールディングに任せることにした。

"'I will take care of your pawnshop,' Spaulding broke in.

"Now, a pawnshop is busy mostly on Thursday and Friday evenings, just before payday. So I thought I could work midday at the office with Mr. Ross. And I knew that Spaulding could take care of the shop.

(182 [1,411] words)

✤ KEYWORDS

- ☐ **crowd** [kráʊd]
- ☐ **Duncan Ross** [dʌ́ŋkən rɔ́:s]
- ☐ *Dear me!*
- ☐ **organization** [ɔ̀:ʳgənəzéɪʃən]
- ☐ *so that*
- ☐ **unusually** [ənjú:ʒwəli]
- ☐ *break in*
- ☐ **payday** [péɪdèɪ]
- ☐ **midday** [míddèɪ]
- ☐ *take care of*

✤ KEY SENTENCES (☞ p. 85)

16 Then • he opened the door • and shouted • to the crowd • that the job was taken.

17 This money was given • to our organization • so that • more red-headed sons • could be born.

"'That is fine,' I said. 'And what is the work?'

"'It's very easy. But you have to be in the office, or at least in the building, the whole time. If you leave, you lose the job forever.'

"'But for only four hours a day? That is not a problem.'

"'No excuse will be allowed.'

"'And the work?'

"'To copy the Encyclopedia Britannica. You must bring your own paper and pen. But we will give you a desk and chair. Can you start tomorrow?'

"'Yes.'

"'Then, goodbye, Mr. Wilson, and congratulations.'

"I was very pleased with my new job. But I thought about it later and I began to feel bad about it.

仕事は百科事典を写すことだった。後でウィルソンは何かのトリックに違いないと思って嫌な気分になったが、朝、インクと紙を買い事務所に行った。

"I thought it must be some trick. [18]Who would pay someone so much money for doing such easy work? In the morning, however, I bought a bottle of ink and some paper and went over to Mr. Ross's office.

(152 [1,563] words)

✤ KEYWORDS

- ☐ **least** [lí:st]
- ☐ *at least*
- ☐ **whole** [hóʊl]
- ☐ **allow** [əláʊ]
- ☐ **copy** [kɑ́:pi]
- ☐ **encyclopedia** [ɪnsàɪkləpí:di:ə]
- ☐ **Encyclopedia Britannica** [ɪnsàɪkləpí:di:ə brɪtǽnɪkə]
- ☐ **congratulations** [kəngrætʃəléɪʃənz]
- ☐ **trick** [trík]
- ☐ **ink** [íŋk]
- ☐ *go over to*

✤ KEY SENTENCES (☞ p. 85)

[18]Who would pay someone • so much money • for doing such easy work?

"The table was ready for me. Mr. Duncan came into my room from time to time. [19]At two o'clock, he said good-bye and was pleased that I had copied so many pages.

"This continued for a long time. Every Saturday, Mr. Duncan gave me four gold coins. [20]Every morning I came in at ten and every afternoon I left at two. Eight weeks passed like this. Then, suddenly the whole business came to an end."

"To an end?" I asked.

"Yes, sir. It was just this morning. I went to my work as usual, but the door was shut and locked. This note was hanging on the door":

The Red-Headed League
is
Dissolved.
October 9, 1890

(116 [1,679] words)

その後仕事は順調に８週間続いたが、今朝いつものように職場に行くとドアが閉まっていて「赤毛組合は解散した」と書かれたメモがかかっていた。

✤ KEYWORDS

- ☐ *from time to time*
- ☐ **gold** [góʊld]
- ☐ *come to an end*
- ☐ **usual** [júːʒuːəl]
- ☐ **shut** [ʃʌ́t]
- ☐ **lock** [lάːk]
- ☐ **hang** [hǽŋ]
- ☐ **dissolve** [dɪzάːlv]

✤ KEY SENTENCES (☞ p. 86)

19 At two o'clock, • he said good-bye • and was pleased • that I had copied • so many pages.

20 Every morning • I came in • at ten • and every afternoon • I left • at two.

[21]Sherlock Holmes and I both read the note again and then broke out laughing.

"I do not think it is funny," Mr. Wilson said. "I can go somewhere else if you are going to laugh."

"No, please don't go," said Holmes. "It is just so unusual. Tell us, what did you do when you found this note?"

"[22]I went down to the ground floor and asked the owner of the building what had happened to the Red-headed League. He said that he had never heard of any such league. Then I asked him who Mr. Duncan Ross was.

"'Oh, he was a lawyer,' he told me. 'He was using the room upstairs until his new office was ready. At 17 King Edward Street.'

"I went to that address, Mr. Holmes, but it was a different company and I could not find Mr. Ross."

ホームズと私は笑い、ウィルソンが他に行くと言うのをホームズは止めた。
ウィルソンは引っ越し先に行ったがロス氏を見つけられなかったという。

"What did you do then?"

"I asked Spaulding to help me, but he did not know what else to do. So I have come to you for help."

(171 [1,850] words)

✤ KEYWORDS

- ☐ *break out laughing*
- ☐ **somewhere** [sʌ́mwèəʳ]
- ☐ **owner** [óʊnəʳ]
- ☐ **lawyer** [lɔ́ɪəʳ]
- ☐ **upstairs** [əpstéəʳz]
- ☐ **King Edward Street** [kíŋ édwəʳd strí:t]
- ☐ **address** [ædrés]

✤ KEY SENTENCES (☞ p. 86)

21 Sherlock Holmes and I • both read the note again • and then • broke out laughing.

22 I went down • to the ground floor • and asked the owner • of the building • what had happened • to the Red-headed League.

"I am happy to look into your case. I think it may be more serious than you expect. [23]How long had you known your assistant Spaulding before he found this advertisement?"

"About a month. He answered an advertisement I put in the paper."

"Why did you pick him?"

"Because he only wanted half pay."

"Are his ears pierced for earrings?"

"Yes."

"Are you satisfied with his work while you are gone?"

"Yes, there is not much to do during the day."

"That will be all for now, Mr. Wilson. Today is Saturday. On Monday I will give you my opinion."

[24]"Well, Watson," said Holmes when Mr. Wilson had gone, "what do you think?"

ホームズは、ウィルソンにスポールディングのことについていくつか尋ねた。ウィルソンが去ったあと、ホームズは私をコンサートに誘った。

"I cannot understand it at all," I said.

"Yes, it is very strange," he said. "There is a concert this afternoon. Can you come, Doctor?"

"Yes. I am never busy on Saturday."

"Then, let us take lunch on the way. Come along."

(155 [2,005] words)

✤ KEYWORDS

- ☐ *look into*
- ☐ **expect** [ɪkspékt]
- ☐ **assistant** [əsístənt]
- ☐ **pierced** [píəʳst]
- ☐ **earring** [íərɪŋ]
- ☐ **satisfied** [sǽtɪsfàɪd]
- ☐ *That is all for now.*
- ☐ *not ~ at all*
- ☐ **concert** [kɑ́ːnsəʳt]
- ☐ *on the way*
- ☐ *come along*

✤ KEY SENTENCES (☞ p. 86)

23 How long • had you known • your assistant Spaulding • before he found this advertisement?

24 "Well, Watson," • said Holmes • when Mr. Wilson had gone, • "what do you think?"

[25]We took the subway to Aldersgate, then walked a short way to the small building that Mr. Wilson had told us about. We saw a brown sign with JABEZ WILSON written in white letters. This was the pawnshop. Holmes walked up and down the street, studying the buildings. [26]Then he walked up the street to the pawnshop and knocked at the door. A young man opened the door and asked us to come in.

"Thank you. I would just like to ask the way to the Strand from here."

"Third right, fourth left," said the assistant, closing the door.

"Smart man," Holmes said. "Fourth-smartest man in London."

"I am sure that he is important in our mystery. You wanted to see him, didn't you?" I asked.

(126 [2,131] words)

地下鉄でアルダーズゲートに行き、少し歩くとウィルソンの質屋があった。ホームズは質屋のドアをノックして、ドアを開けた若い男に道を尋ねた。

✤ KEYWORDS

- ☐ **subway** [sʌ́bwèɪ]
- ☐ **Aldersgate** [ɔ́:ldəʳzgèɪt]
- ☐ **knock** [nɑ́:k]
- ☐ **Strand** [strǽnd]
- ☐ **smart** [smɑ́:ʳt]
- ☐ **mystery** [místəri]

✤ KEY SENTENCES (☞ p. 86)

25 We took the subway • to Aldersgate, • then walked a short way • to the small building • that Mr. Wilson had told us about.

26 Then he walked up the street • to the pawnshop • and knocked at the door.

"Not him, the knees of his trousers."

"What did you see?"

"My dear doctor, we cannot talk here. We are spies in an enemy's country."

[27]We turned the corner, we were on one of the most expensive streets in London.

"Just a minute," said Holmes. "I am trying to learn all the buildings in this neighborhood."

After a few minutes, he said, "Now, Doctor, we have done our work. Let us have some lunch, then we shall listen to sweet music."

Holmes enjoyed music completely. I never knew anybody who loved music more than him. [28]Sometimes, it seemed that listening to music helped him solve his most difficult mysteries.

After the concert, Holmes asked me to come back later that night.

角を曲がると、そこはロンドンでも最も高級な通りだった。コンサート後、ホームズは私に、銃をポケットに忍ばせて10時に来てほしいと言った。

"I will need your help with something," he said. "Come at ten o'clock. And, Doctor, there may be some danger, so put your gun in your pocket."

(148 [2,279] words)

✤ KEYWORDS

- ☐ **knee** [níː]
- ☐ **trousers** [tráuzəʳz]
- ☐ **spy** [spáɪ]
- ☐ **enemy** [énəmi]
- ☐ **neighborhood** [néɪbəʳhùd]
- ☐ **music** [mjúːzɪk]
- ☐ **completely** [kəmplíːtli]
- ☐ **anybody** [éniːbədi]
- ☐ **gun** [gʌ́n]

✤ KEY SENTENCES (☞ p. 86)

[27] We turned the corner, • we were • on one of the most expensive streets • in London.

[28] Sometimes, • it seemed • that listening to music • helped him solve • his most difficult mysteries.

[29]I did not understand what our business was that night. Where were we going? What were we going to do? [30]I couldn't understand anything, even though I had seen and heard every piece of evidence that Holmes had.

When I arrived at his rooms later that night, he was talking loudly with two men. One was a policeman.

"Ah, Watson!" cried Holmes. "Let me introduce my friend from Scotland Yard. He is joining us tonight."

The other man was a Mr. Merryweather. He did not look happy.

"I am very sorry to be here," said Mr. Merryweather. "I always play cards with my friends on Saturday nights."

"I think you will find the game tonight more exciting," Holmes said. "We are looking for

夜、ホームズの部屋に到着すると一人の警官とメリーウェザー氏が先に来ていた。ホームズは、今夜は英国犯罪組織のトップを探していると言った。

England's head of crime."

"John Clay," the policeman said. "He is young but very smart. He studied at Oxford. I've been looking for him for years. I hope you are right about tonight, Holmes."

(157 [2,436] words)

✤ KEYWORDS

- ☐ **evidence** [évədəns]
- ☐ **policeman** [pəlíːsmən]
- ☐ **Scotland Yard** [skάːtlənd jάːʳd]
- ☐ **Merryweather** [mèriwéðəʳ]
- ☐ *play cards*
- ☐ **England** [íŋglənd]
- ☐ **John Clay** [dʒάːn kléɪ]
- ☐ **Oxford** [άːksfəʳd]
- ☐ *look for*

✤ KEY SENTENCES (☞ p. 87)

29 I did not understand • what our business was • that night.

30 I couldn't understand anything, • even though • I had seen and heard • every piece of evidence • that Holmes had.

We caught a cab and Holmes told the driver where to go.

During the drive, Holmes explained to me why he brought the two men. “Merryweather is personally interested in this case. Jones is a good, brave policeman.”

When we got out of the cab, Mr. Merryweather led us down a small street. We entered a large underground room filled with large boxes.

“A strong room,” Holmes said.

“Yes,” Merryweather said, hitting his stick on the floor. “Why, it sounds quite empty,” he said, looking up in shock.

[31]“I must ask you to be quiet, Mr. Merryweather.”

タクシーを降り、メリーウェザー氏に案内された地下の部屋は、ロンドン最大級の銀行の金庫室だった。メリーウェザー氏は銀行の重要人物だった。

Holmes got down on the floor and began looking at the cracks between the stones. After a few minutes, he jumped up.

"We have to wait an hour," he said. "After Mr. Wilson has gone to bed, they will work fast. [32]Watson, you must know that we are in the basement of one of the largest banks in London. Merryweather is an important man at this bank. He will explain why criminals are interested in this place."

(174 [2,610] words)

✤ KEYWORDS

- ☐ **driver** [dráɪvəʳ]
- ☐ **Jones** [dʒóʊnz]
- ☐ *get out of*
- ☐ **cab** [kǽb]
- ☐ *lead someone down*
- ☐ **underground** [ʌ́ndəʳgràʊnd]
- ☐ *strong room*
- ☐ **stick** [stík]
- ☐ *in shock*
- ☐ *get down*
- ☐ **crack** [krǽk]
- ☐ **stone** [stóʊn]
- ☐ **basement** [béɪsmənt]
- ☐ **criminal** [krímənəl]
- ☐ **place** [pléɪs]

✤ KEY SENTENCES (☞ p. 87)

[31] "I must ask you • to be quiet, • Mr. Merryweather."

[32] Watson, • you must know • that we are in the basement • of one of the largest banks • in London.

"It is our French gold," Merryweather whispered to me. "Some months ago we bought 30,000 coins from the Bank of France. They are here, in these boxes," he said, pointing all around.

"We must sit in the dark now," Holmes said. "It is too dangerous to light the room. When they come, they may open fire. If they do, Watson, you must shoot them."

The dark room was very tense as we waited for the criminals to come.

"There is only one way of escape. I hope you did as I told you, Jones," Holmes said.

"I sent a chief and two officers to the front door of the house."

"Good. Now we wait."

銀行は数か月前にフランス銀行から３万枚の金貨を購入していた。部屋を真っ暗にして犯人が来るのを待っていると、突然光が見えたような気がした。

[33]To me, it felt as though we waited the whole night, but I learned later that it was only a little more than an hour. Suddenly, I thought I saw some light.

(147 [2,757] words)

✤ KEYWORDS

- ☐ **French** [fréntʃ]
- ☐ **whisper** [ʰwíspəʳ]
- ☐ **France** [frǽns]
- ☐ *all around*
- ☐ *open fire*
- ☐ **tense** [téns]
- ☐ **escape** [ɪskéɪp]
- ☐ *way of escape*
- ☐ **chief** [tʃíːf]
- ☐ **officer** [ɔ́ːfɪsəʳ]
- ☐ *as though*

✤ KEY SENTENCES (☞ p. 87)

[33]To me, • it felt • as though • we waited the whole night, • but I learned later • that it was only a little more • than an hour.

First it was a spot, then it became a yellow line. Then a hand came out of the floor, and went back in again. All was quiet. 34 Soon some stones were thrown aside and a young man's face looked into the room. He climbed up. Another man followed him. He had very red hair.

"It's all clear. Have you got the bags, Archie? Jump!"

"Give up, John Clay," said Holmes. 35 "We've got you, and there are three men waiting for him at the door."

The young man looked shocked. Then his face turned into a sneer. "How clever you are. I must compliment you."

"And I, you. Your red-headed idea was very unique."

(113 [2,870] words)

床から若い男が、続いて赤毛の男が現れた。「あきらめろ、ジョン・クレイ」ホームズが言った。「君の赤毛のアイデアはとてもユニークだったよ」

✤ KEYWORDS

- ☐ **spot** [spɑ́:t]
- ☐ **line** [láɪn]
- ☐ **aside** [əsáɪd]
- ☐ *throw aside*
- ☐ *look into*
- ☐ **Archie** [ɑ́:ʳtʃi]
- ☐ *give up*
- ☐ *turn into*
- ☐ **sneer** [sníəʳ]
- ☐ **clever** [klévəʳ]
- ☐ **compliment** [kɑ́:mpləment]

✤ KEY SENTENCES (☞ p. 87)

34 Soon • some stones were thrown aside • and a young man's face • looked into the room.

35 "We've got you, • and there are three men • waiting for him • at the door."

"All right," said Jones. "We've got you. Now march you're going to prison."

John Clay walked to the police car.

"Really, Mr. Holmes," said Mr. Merryweather. "I don't know how the bank can thank you or repay you. You have stopped one of the biggest bank robberies that I have ever heard of."

"I have been after John Clay for a long time, and I am glad he was caught at last. I quite enjoyed this case, because the story told by Mr. Wilson was very interesting."

Later that night, Holmes explained the mystery to me.

"[36]The criminals simply wanted to get Mr. Wilson out of the way for a few hours every day. John Clay thought of the plan, and his friend interviewed the red-headed men. [37]When I heard the assistant was working for

メリーウェザー氏は「どれだけ感謝したらいいかわかりません」とホームズに言った。その夜、私は彼にどうやって計画を推測できたのかを尋ねた。

half pay, I thought he must have a reason."

"But how could you guess what his plan was?" I asked.

(155 [3,025] words)

✤ KEYWORDS

☐ **prison** [prízən]
☐ **repay** [ripéɪ]
☐ **robbery** [rɑ́:bəri]
☐ *at last*
☐ *get ~ out of the way*

✤ KEY SENTENCES (☞ p. 87)

36 The criminals simply wanted • to get Mr. Wilson • out of the way • for a few hours • every day.

37 When I heard • the assistant was working • for half pay, • I thought • he must have a reason.

“[38]When I heard that he spent hours in the basement, I thought he must be making a tunnel to another building. When I went to the door of the pawnshop, I saw the knees of his trousers. They were dark from digging. Then as we walked the surrounding streets, I saw the bank. After the concert, I called Scotland Yard and the bank director. That is why the two gentlemen came with us.”

“But how did you know they would try the crime tonight?”

“Well, this morning they put the sign on the door. [39]They did not care if Mr. Wilson was in his store or not. That meant they had finished their tunnel. But they had to use it as soon as possible, before the gold was moved. [40]Saturday would be best because they had two days when the bank was closed. So I expected them tonight.”

「彼が地下で過ごしていると聞きトンネルを作っていると思った。ドアのサインは完成を意味し、実行は銀行の休日が２日ある土曜の夜だと予測した」

"Your reasoning is wonderful!"

"It saves me from boredom," he answered, yawning.

(160 [3,185] words)

✤ KEYWORDS

☐ **tunnel** [tʌ́nəl]
☐ **digging** [dígɪŋ]
☐ **director** [dəréktəʳ]
☐ **possible** [pɑ́:səbəl]
☐ **boredom** [bɔ́:ʳdəm]
☐ **yawn** [jɔ́:n]

✤ KEY SENTENCES (☞ p. 87–88)

38 When I heard • that he spent hours • in the basement, • I thought • he must be making a tunnel • to another building.

39 They did not care • if Mr. Wilson was • in his store or not.

40 Saturday would be best • because they had two days • when the bank was closed.

The Adventure of the Speckled Band

まだらの紐

04 [41]Early in April of 1883, I found Sherlock Holmes standing next to my bed waiting for me to wake up. It was still seven o'clock in the morning, and he usually slept late.

"Sorry to wake you up so early, Watson."

"What? Is there a fire?"

"No, a young lady is here to see me. [42]When young ladies wake people early in the morning, there must be something very important to talk about. I thought you would like to listen too."

"Oh, yes!" I replied, getting up and quickly dressing.

I love following Holmes's work and watching his quick mind solve a case. The young lady was dressed in black and had a veil over her face. When we entered the room, she stood up.

目覚めると私のベッドの隣にホームズが立っていた。「朝早くに若い女性が来た。重要な話に違いない。君も聞いてみたいだろう」私はすぐに着替えた。

"Good morning, madam," said Holmes. "My name is Sherlock Holmes. This is my friend, Dr. Watson. Oh, I see that you are shaking. Come close to the fire."

(153 [3,338] words)

✤ KEYWORDS

- ☐ **speckled** [spékəld]
- ☐ **band** [bǽnd]
- ☐ **reply** [rɪpláɪ]
- ☐ *get up*
- ☐ **mind** [máɪnd]
- ☐ *dressed in black*
- ☐ **veil** [véɪl]
- ☐ **madam** [mǽdəm]

✤ KEY SENTENCES (☞ p. 88)

41 Early in April of 1883, • I found Sherlock Holmes • standing next to my bed • waiting for me • to wake up.

42 When young ladies wake people • early in the morning, • there must be • something very important • to talk about.

"It is not cold which makes me shake. It is fear, Mr. Holmes."

[43]She took off the veil and we could see that her face was pale, with frightened eyes. She looked like a hunted animal. She seemed to be about thirty years old, but she looked even older. Holmes studied her quickly.

"Do not fear," he said kindly, touching her arm. "We will make everything all right. I see that you have just arrived by train."

"How did you know that?"

"I see the half of a return ticket in your glove. You must have left home very early."

"You are right," she said. "[44]I left home before six this morning and got the first train to Waterloo. Sir, I cannot take this any longer! I have heard of you, Mr. Holmes, and how you help people. Please help me. I cannot pay you

彼女の顔は青白く目は怯えていた。ホームズは「恐れることはありません」と優しく言った。「今朝一番列車で来ました。どうか私を助けてください」

now, but in six weeks I will be married, and I will be able to pay you then."

(163 [3,501] words)

✤ KEYWORDS

- ☐ **fear** [fíəʳ]
- ☐ *take off*
- ☐ **pale** [péɪl]
- ☐ **frightened** [fráɪtənd]
- ☐ **hunted** [hʌ́ntəd]
- ☐ *seem to be*
- ☐ **Waterloo** [wɔ́ːtəʳlùː]
- ☐ *any longer*
- ☐ **married** [mérid]

✤ KEY SENTENCES (☞ p. 88)

43 She took off the veil • and we could see • that her face was pale, • with frightened eyes.

44 I left home • before six • this morning • and got the first train • to Waterloo.

"Don't worry about payment. [45]Now, please give us the information that will make it possible to help you."

"Oh," she cried, "but I am afraid of such small things! [46]Even that one person who could help me thinks that my problems are in my own mind. But I believe that you, Mr. Holmes, can see deeper. You will be able to tell me how to walk through the dangers I face."

"I will try, madam."

"My name is Helen Stoner. I live with my stepfather. My family was once the richest family in England, but my grandfather wasted our money. Now we only have an old house with a heavy mortgage. My stepfather is a doctor. He worked in India. While he was there, his servant robbed him, so he beat him very badly. He was sent to prison, and he returned to England years later. He is not a happy man.

(152 [3,653] words)

女性の名はヘレン・ストーナー。医者の義父と二人暮らし。家は裕福だったが今は見る影もない。義父はインドで召使いを殴り服役した後に帰国した。

✤ KEYWORDS

- ☐ **payment** [péɪmənt]
- ☐ *even that*
- ☐ *walk through the dangers*
- ☐ **Helen Stoner** [hélən stóʊnə^{r}]
- ☐ **stepfather** [stépfɑ̀ːðə^{r}]
- ☐ **mortgage** [mɔ́ː^{r}gədʒ]
- ☐ **India** [índiə]
- ☐ **servant** [sə́ː^{r}vənt]
- ☐ **rob** [rɑ́ːb]
- ☐ **beat** [bíːt]

✤ KEY SENTENCES (☞ p. 88)

45 Now, • please give us the information • that will make it possible • to help you.

46 Even that • one person • who could help me • thinks • that my problems are • in my own mind.

"Later, my mother married our stepfather. 47 She gave him all of her money, with a note that some of the money would go to me and my sister when we were married. My mother died about eight years ago in a train accident, but we had enough money to live comfortably with him. 48 When my mother died, he took us to live in his family house in the country. My sister and I were always very close and enjoyed each other's company there.

"But my stepfather often became angry. He fought with everyone. Twice the police had to come to our house. Last week, he hurt a man badly and I had to give him money to keep him quiet. My stepfather has no friends except the traveling gypsies. Sometimes they come to live on our land in their tents. Sometimes my stepfather leaves our home to travel with them.

(150 [3,803] words)

母は義父に、娘らが結婚したときに分ける条件で財産を渡していた。その後母は事故で亡くなり、義父は彼女と妹を連れて田舎の実家に引っ越した。

✤ KEYWORDS

- ☐ **accident** [ǽksədənt]
- ☐ **comfortably** [kʌ́mfəʳtəbli]
- ☐ *enjoy each other's company*
- ☐ **angry** [ǽŋgri]
- ☐ **except** [ıksépt]
- ☐ **gypsy** [dʒípsi]
- ☐ **tent** [tént]

✤ KEY SENTENCES (☞ p. 88)

47 She gave him • all of her money, • with a note • that some of the money • would go to me • and my sister • when we were married.

48 When my mother died, • he took us • to live • in his family house • in the country.

"So you see my sister and I were quite unhappy. No servant would stay in our house. We did all the work. Finally, my sister died. She was only thirty years old, but her hair was already completely white."

"Your sister is dead?"

"She died two years ago. [49]That is what I have come to talk to you about. We had few friends. Sometimes we went to see my mother's sister near Harrow. [50]My sister went there at Christmas two years ago and met a nice man. They got engaged. But just before the wedding took place, I lost her."

Until this time, Holmes had had his eyes closed. But at this point, he opened them and looked at his visitor.

"Please explain the details."

姉は２年前、結婚式の直前に亡くなっていた。家は古く、その片側に住み、父と姉、ミス・ストーナーは同じ廊下に面して並ぶ部屋を寝室にしていた。

"Our house is old, as I said. We lived in only one side of it. My father's bedroom was first, my sister's second, and mine, the third. All the doors open into the same hallway."

(160 [3,963] words)

✤ KEYWORDS

- ☐ **unhappy** [ənhǽpi]
- ☐ *talk to someone about*
- ☐ **Harrow** [hǽroʊ]
- ☐ **Christmas** [krísməs]
- ☐ **engaged** [ɪngéɪdʒd]
- ☐ **wedding** [wédɪŋ]
- ☐ *take place*
- ☐ **visitor** [vízɪtəʳ]
- ☐ **bedroom** [bédrù:m]
- ☐ *open into*
- ☐ **hallway** [hɔ́:lwèɪ]

✤ KEY SENTENCES (☞ p. 88–89)

49 That is • what • I have come • to talk to you about.

50 My sister went there • at Christmas • two years ago • and met a nice man.

"I see."

"That night, my father had gone to his bedroom early. [51]But my sister could smell his cigars, which she didn't like, so she came into my room. We talked for a long time about her upcoming wedding, then she stood up to go.

"[52]'Tell me, Helen,' she said, 'have you ever heard anyone whistle late at night?'

"'Never,' I said.

"'The last few nights, about three o'clock in the morning, I hear someone whistling. It wakes me up. I thought maybe you had heard it, too.'

"'No, it must be the gypsies on our land.'

"'Yes, maybe.' And she went into her room and locked the door."

"Did you always lock your doors at night?" Holmes asked.

ある晩ミス・ストーナーの部屋を訪れた姉は、夜中に口笛の音が聞こえると言った後、自室に戻った。眠れなかった彼女は夜遅くに姉の悲鳴を聞いた。

"Yes." She paused, then continued her story.

"I could not sleep that night. It was raining, and late at night I heard my sister scream." She stopped again and shivered.

(149 [4,112] words)

✤ KEYWORDS

- □ **cigar** [sɪgɑ́:ʳ]
- □ **upcoming** [ʌ́pkʌ̀mɪŋ]
- □ **whistle** [ʰwísəl]
- □ **lock** [lɑ́:k]
- □ **pause** [pɔ́:z]
- □ **scream** [skrí:m]
- □ **shiver** [ʃívəʳ]

✤ KEY SENTENCES (☞ p. 89)

51 But my sister could smell his cigars, • which she didn't like, • so she came into my room.

52 'Tell me, Helen,' • she said, • 'have you ever heard • anyone whistle • late at night?'

"I ran from my bed. [53]I heard a whistle like she had described and then the sound of some metal falling. I ran down the hall to my sister's door. My sister ran out of her room. Her face was white and her body was shaking. She fell to the ground and I held her in my arms. She said, 'Helen! It was the band! The speckled band!' She tried to say something else, but could not. She pointed to our father's room, then she died. My father came running from his room and tried to help her, but it was too late."

"One moment," said Holmes, "are you sure about this whistle and metallic sound?"

[54]"Well, I think I heard it but there was such a terrible storm, maybe it was in my head."

"Was your sister dressed?"

"She was in her bedclothes. In her right hand was a match, and in her left a matchbox."

(157 [4,269] words)

姉の部屋に向かうと姉が真っ白な顔で飛び出し「まだらの紐よ」と言い、義父の部屋を指差し死んだ。彼が部屋から助けに出てきたときには遅すぎた。

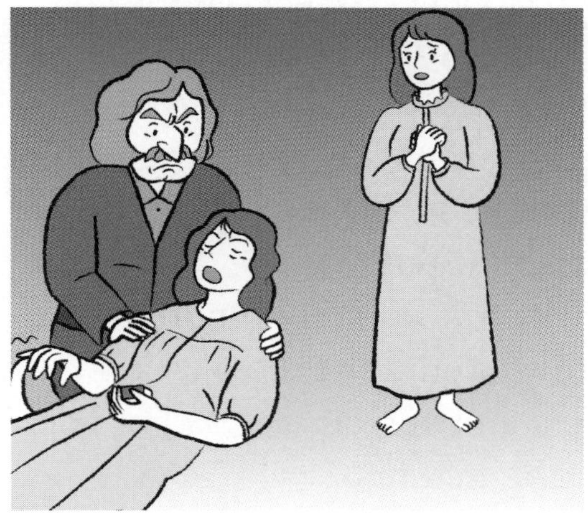

✤ KEYWORDS

- ☐ **describe** [dɪskráɪb]
- ☐ **metal** [métəl]
- ☐ *fall to the ground*
- ☐ *hold someone in one's arms*
- ☐ *come running from*
- ☐ **moment** [móʊmənt]
- ☐ *(be) sure about*
- ☐ **metallic** [mətǽlɪk]
- ☐ **storm** [stɔ́ːʳm]
- ☐ **bedclothes** [bèdklóʊðz]
- ☐ **matchbox** [mǽtʃbɑ̀ːks]

✤ KEY SENTENCES (☞ p. 89)

53 I heard a whistle • like she had described • and then • the sound • of some metal falling.

54 "Well, • I think I heard it • but there was such a terrible storm, • maybe it was • in my head."

"So she was lighting a match when the accident happened. What did the coroner say?"

"He could not find any cause for death. I know that the door and the windows were locked. My sister was alone in her room. And there were no marks of violence on her body."

"How about poison?"

"The doctors could find nothing."

"Then what did she die of?"

55 "Of fear and nervous shock, but I don't know what frightened her."

"Were there gypsies on your land then?"

"Yes, there are almost always some there."

56 "What do you think she meant by the 'speckled band'?"

"I don't know. Maybe a band of people, maybe a kind of handkerchief."

Holmes shook his head. He seemed to disagree.

検死官も医者も死因がわからず、「まだらの紐」も謎だった。姉の死後ミス・ストーナーは寂しく暮らすが、一か月前に友人から結婚を申し込まれる。

"Please continue."

"After my sister's death, my life has been very lonely. A month ago, a dear friend asked me to marry him.

(144 [4,413] words)

✤ KEYWORDS

- ☐ **coroner** [kɔ́:rənə^r]
- ☐ **death** [déθ]
- ☐ **mark** [mɑ́:^rk]
- ☐ **violence** [váɪələns]
- ☐ **poison** [pɔ́ɪzən]
- ☐ *die of*
- ☐ **frighten** [fráɪtən]
- ☐ *mean A by B*
- ☐ **handkerchief** [hǽŋkə^rtʃɪf]
- ☐ **disagree** [dɪsəgrí:]
- ☐ **lonely** [lóʊnli]
- ☐ **marry** [méri]

✤ KEY SENTENCES (☞ p. 89)

55 "Of fear and nervous shock, • but I don't know • what frightened her."

56 "What do you think • she meant • by the 'speckled band'?"

"My stepfather is not against our plan. We hope to be married in the spring. My stepfather is fixing our house, and two days ago, the builders started working on my room, so I moved into my sister's bedroom. I was sleeping in her bed last night. [57]Imagine how frightened I was when I heard the whistle that she heard before her death. I lit a lamp, but there was nothing in my room. [58]I got the train first thing this morning to visit you and ask for your advice."

"That is good, but have you told me everything?"

"Yes, all."

"Miss Stoner, you have not. You are protecting your father." Holmes pushed back the arm of her dress and showed bruises on her arm.

家の修繕で業者がミス・ストーナーの部屋の工事を始め、彼女は姉の寝室に引っ越した。昨夜姉のベッドで寝ていた彼女は口笛を聞き恐怖に襲われる。

"He treats you cruelly."

At this, she turned red. "He does not mean to hurt me."

(141 [4,554] words)

✤ KEYWORDS

- ☐ **fix** [fíks]
- ☐ **builder** [bíldəʳ]
- ☐ *move into*
- ☐ **lit** [lít] < light
- ☐ **lamp** [lǽmp]
- ☐ *first thing*
- ☐ *push back*
- ☐ **bruise** [brúːz]
- ☐ **treat** [tríːt]
- ☐ **cruelly** [krúːli]

✤ KEY SENTENCES (☞ p. 89)

57 Imagine • how frightened I was • when I heard the whistle • that she heard • before her death.

58 I got the train • first thing • this morning • to visit you • and ask for your advice.

Holmes looked into the fire. "[59]There are more details I wish to know. We must act quickly. Will your father be home today? I would like to see the rooms without him knowing."

"He will be out of the house all day today."

"Will you come, Watson?"

"Of course."

"I have some things to do in London," said Miss Stoner. "[60]But I will return by the noon train to be there in time for your arrival."

"Then you may expect us in the early afternoon. Will you stay now and join us for breakfast?"

"No, I must go. I feel better now that I have talked to you." She dropped the veil over her face and left the room quietly.

"What do you think, Watson?"

「父親に知られずに部屋を見たい」と言うホームズは私を誘い、ミス・ストーナーと現地で会う約束をする。気分が落ち着いた彼女は部屋を出た。

"I don't know! What were those whistles? And the 'speckled band'?"

"The band could be the gypsies, or the metal band on the window. But I cannot understand anything. That is why we are going to visit the house today."

(165 [4,719] words)

✤ KEYWORDS

☐ *in time for* ☐ **arrival** [əráɪvəl]

✤ KEY SENTENCES (☞ p. 89–90)

59 There are more details • I wish to know.

60 "But I will return • by the noon train • to be there • in time • for your arrival."

[61]Just then a huge man with an evil face entered our room.

"Which of you is Holmes?" he demanded.

"I am," Holmes said.

"I am Dr. Roylott. Why did my daughter come to see you? What did she say?" he yelled.

Holmes only smiled.

"I know you are a troublemaker! You better not make trouble for me. I am a dangerous man," Roylott said. He picked up an iron fire poker and bent it in half. "See that this does not happen to you." And he left the room.

"What a friendly person," Holmes said, laughing. [62]"Now we will have breakfast, Watson, and then I will go to the hospital where I will try to get some information before we take the train."

(123 [4,842] words)

邪悪な顔の大男が部屋に入ってきた。自分はロイロット博士だと名乗り、ホームズに面倒を起こすなと警告して鉄の火かき棒を半分に折り曲げた。

✤ KEYWORDS

- ☐ **huge** [hjúːdʒ]
- ☐ **evil** [íːvəl]
- ☐ **demand** [dɪmǽnd]
- ☐ **Roylott** [rɔ̀ɪlɑ́ːt]
- ☐ **troublemaker** [trʌ́bəlmèɪkə^r]
- ☐ *better not*
- ☐ **iron** [áɪə^{r}n]
- ☐ **poker** [póʊkə^r]
- ☐ **bent** [bént] < bend
- ☐ *in half*
- ☐ *see that*

✤ KEY SENTENCES (☞ p. 90)

61 Just then • a huge man • with an evil face • entered our room.

62 "Now • we will have breakfast, • Watson, • and then • I will go • to the hospital • where I will try • to get some information • before we take the train."

It was almost one o'clock when Holmes returned. He had a sheet of paper with a lot of numbers written on it.

"I have seen the will of Dr. Roylott's late wife. [63]The income is now only 750 pounds a year, which means that in the case of marriage each daughter gets 250 pounds. That means that this fine man would have almost no money if both daughters married. He has strong reasons for preventing the girls from marrying. Now, Watson, we must leave immediately. [64]I would be very grateful if you would put your gun in your pocket. That and our toothbrushes are all that we need to take."

It was a sunny day and we reached the house easily. We were taking a cab from the train station to the house when we saw a young lady walking over the fields toward the house.

ロイロット博士の妻の遺言によると、娘が２人とも結婚すると彼の分のお金がほとんどなくなる。彼には娘たちの結婚を阻止する強い動機があった。

"Is that Miss Stoner?" Holmes said. "Let's join her."

We got out of the cab and went across the fields toward her. Her face was full of joy when she saw us.

(178 [5,020] words)

✤ KEYWORDS

- ☐ **sheet** [ʃíːt]
- ☐ **will** [wíl]
- ☐ **late** [léɪt]
- ☐ **income** [ínkʌ̀m]
- ☐ *in the case of*
- ☐ **marriage** [mérɪdʒ]
- ☐ *fine man*
- ☐ **prevent** [prɪvént]
- ☐ **immediately** [ìmíːdìːətli]
- ☐ **grateful** [gréɪtfəl]
- ☐ **toothbrush** [túːθbrəʃ]
- ☐ **joy** [dʒɔ́ɪ]

✤ KEY SENTENCES (☞ p. 90)

63 The income is • now only 750 pounds • a year, • which means that • in the case of marriage • each daughter gets 250 pounds.

64 I would be very grateful • if you would put your gun • in your pocket.

"I am so glad you could come. Dr. Roylott will not be back until evening."

"We have already met the good man," Holmes said, explaining the morning's event.

"Good heavens! He has followed me then. What shall I do?"

"You must be very careful. 65 If he is angry with you tonight, we shall take you away to your aunt's at Harrow. But now, we must use our time wisely."

66 The building was old with broken windows covered with wooden boards. Blue smoke curled above into the sky. Some workmen were present. Holmes walked around the old house slowly.

"These are the bedrooms?"

"Yes."

"Are there windows?"

ミス・ストーナーは、ホームズと私が義父と会ったと知って驚く。ホームズは家の外から寝室を確認した。窓は小さく、外からは開けられなかった。

"Yes, but too small for anyone to pass."

"I see. Please go into your sister's bedroom and close the windows tightly."

Miss Stoner did so. Holmes tried to open the windows but could not. Even a knife could not be passed through. "I cannot figure out how anyone could enter the room. We must look inside."

(162 [5,182] words)

✤ KEYWORDS

- ☐ **heaven** [hévən]
- ☐ *Good heavens!*
- ☐ **wisely** [wáɪzli]
- ☐ **board** [bɔ́ːʳd]
- ☐ **smoke** [smóʊk]
- ☐ **curl** [kə́ːʳl]
- ☐ **workman** [wə́ːʳkmən]
- ☐ **present** [prézənt]
- ☐ **bedroom** [bédrùːm]
- ☐ **tightly** [táɪtli]
- ☐ **knife** [náɪf]
- ☐ **figure** [fígjəʳ]
- ☐ *pass through*
- ☐ *figure out*

✤ KEY SENTENCES (☞ p. 90)

65 If he is angry with you tonight, • we shall take you away • to your aunt's • at Harrow.

66 The building was old • with broken windows • covered • with wooden boards.

It was a nice little room. There was a small bed, dressing-table, brown chair, and carpet. [67]There was a rope hanging over the bed for the servants' bell.

"Please excuse me," Holmes said, and he threw himself down on the floor to examine the wood. He examined the walls in the same way. Then he pulled on the rope over the bed, but there was no bell. [68]There was also a hole in the ceiling connecting this room to the stepfather's bedroom.

"This is a very strange rope," Holmes said. "We shall now look at the next bedroom."

Dr. Roylott's room was larger. There were many books and a chair beside the bed. There was a safe on a table near the chair.

"What's in here?" Holmes asked, touching the safe.

寝室を調べると、ベッドの上にベルのついていない呼び鈴用のロープが下がっていた。博士の部屋には金庫が置かれ、隣にミルクの入った皿があった。

"Business papers," said Miss Stoner.

"Not a cat?"

"No, what a strange idea!"

"But here is a dish of milk next to it."

(154 [5,336] words)

✤ KEYWORDS

- ☐ **dressing-table** [drèsɪŋtéɪbəl]
- ☐ **carpet** [kɑ́ːʳpət]
- ☐ *throw oneself down on*
- ☐ **examine** [ɪgzǽmɪn]
- ☐ *in the same way*
- ☐ *pull on*
- ☐ **bell** [bél]
- ☐ **ceiling** [síːlɪŋ]
- ☐ **beside** [bɪsáɪd]
- ☐ **safe** [séɪf]

✤ KEY SENTENCES (☞ p. 90)

67 There was a rope • hanging over the bed • for the servants' bell.

68 There was also a hole • in the ceiling • connecting this room • to the stepfather's bedroom.

[69]Then he examined the chair carefully and noticed a dog leash tied to one corner of the bed. “Very unusual, don’t you think, Watson?”

“Yes, very strange.”

“I have seen enough, Miss Stoner. Now, please follow my advice exactly.”

“Of course,” she replied.

“Watson and I will spend the night in your room. You must stay in your old room. Tell your stepfather that you have a headache. Open the windows and put your lamp in the window. [70]Then go to your room even though it is being torn up by the builders. Leave the rest to us.”

“Mr. Holmes, do you already know how my sister died?” she asked.

“I believe I do.”

“Please tell me.”

ベッドに犬の鎖が結ばれているのを見たホームズは、ミス・ストーナーに義父に頭痛がすると伝え、窓を開けランプを置いて自室に行くように言った。

"I must have proof first," said Holmes.

Holmes and I went to the local inn to wait for nightfall. As we waited, Holmes said to me, "Watson, I am afraid to take you with me this evening. It will be quite dangerous."

(159 [5,495] words)

✤ KEYWORDS

- ☐ **notice** [nóʊtɪs]
- ☐ **leash** [líːʃ]
- ☐ **exactly** [ɪgzǽktli]
- ☐ **headache** [hédèɪk]
- ☐ *tear up*
- ☐ *leave the rest to*
- ☐ **proof** [prúːf]
- ☐ **inn** [ín]
- ☐ **nightfall** [náɪtfɔ̀ːl]

✤ KEY SENTENCES (☞ p. 90–91)

69 Then • he examined the chair • carefully • and noticed a dog leash • tied • to one corner of the bed.

70 Then • go to your room • even though • it is being torn up • by the builders.

"Well, if I can help you Holmes, I will go. But I do not know what danger you saw."

"[71]It is strange that after the rope and the hole in the ceiling are added to the room, the woman who sleeps there dies. Did you notice anything strange about the bed?"

"No."

"It was bolted to the floor."

The house became dark about nine o'clock. Soon, we saw a bright light in the bedroom window. [72]It was the lamp Holmes had told Miss Stoner to put there. Holmes and I went to the house and snuck into the room through the open window.

"We must sit in the dark," said Holmes. "Do not fall asleep, Watson. Your life depends on it."

夜９時頃、私たちは部屋に忍び込んだ。深夜、医師の部屋に明かりが灯り、小さな音が聞こえた。ホームズはランプを点け天井の穴に向けて杖を振った。

One, two and three o'clock came and went. Nothing happened. Suddenly there was a light in the doctor's room. Then another half hour passed. Suddenly, we heard a very soft sound, like steam from a kettle. At this, Holmes jumped from the bed, lit the lamp and began waving his cane at the hole in the ceiling.

(178 [5,673] words)

✤ KEYWORDS

- ☐ **bolt** [bóʊlt]
- ☐ **snuck** [snʌ́k] < sneak
- ☐ *sneak into*
- ☐ **asleep** [əslíːp]
- ☐ *fall asleep*
- ☐ **depend** [dɪpénd]
- ☐ **steam** [stíːm]
- ☐ **kettle** [kétəl]
- ☐ **wave** [wéɪv]
- ☐ **cane** [kéɪn]

✤ KEY SENTENCES (☞ p. 91)

71 It is strange • that after • the rope and the hole • in the ceiling • are added • to the room, • the woman • who sleeps there • dies.

72 It was the lamp • Holmes had told Miss Stoner • to put there.

"Do you see it, Watson?" he cried out.

But I saw nothing—only his white, frightened face.

When he stopped, there was a terrible cry from the next room.

"What happened?" I asked.

"It's all over," Holmes replied. "Let's go to the doctor's room."

[73]We found the safe open with Dr. Roylott sitting dead in the chair. [74]He had a whistle in his hand and he was wearing a strange yellow band, with brown speckles, around his head.

"The band, the speckled band!" whispered Holmes.

But it was not cloth. It was a yellow snake that had wound itself around the man's head.

(103 [5,776] words)

隣の部屋から叫び声が聞こえた。行くと、金庫が開いておりロイロット博士が座ったまま死んでいた。手に笛を持ち、まだら模様の紐を頭に巻いていた。

✤ KEYWORDS

- ☐ *cry out*
- ☐ *all over*
- ☐ **speckle** [spékəl]
- ☐ **snake** [snéɪk]
- ☐ **wound** [wáʊnd] < wind
- ☐ **itself** [ìtsélf]

✤ KEY SENTENCES (☞ p. 91)

73 We found the safe open • with Dr. Roylott • sitting dead • in the chair.

74 He had a whistle • in his hand • and • he was wearing a strange yellow band, • with brown speckles, • around his head.

"It is a swamp adder, the deadliest snake in India! Let us put the snake back in his cage and take Miss Stoner to a safe place. Then we must tell the police what happened."

On the train back to London the next day, Holmes told me what had happened.

"[75]I realized that the danger was not from the window or the door, but from the hole in the wall. [76]The bed was bolted to the floor so that the rope could be used as a bridge for something to pass through the wall and come down to the bed. Then the idea of a snake came to me. Only a coroner with very good eyes would see two little holes made by a snake bite. The doctor had trained the snake to go into the next room and come back at the sound of his whistle.

まだらの紐の正体はインドで最も凶暴なヘビだった。博士はロープを橋代わりにヘビを隣の寝室まで送り込み、笛の音で戻るように訓練していたのだ。

"I examined his chair. It was clear that he stood on it. I knew it was a snake when I saw the milk, the leash and the safe.

(175 [5,951] words)

✤ KEYWORDS

- ☐ **swamp adder** [swɑ́ːmp ǽdəʳ]
- ☐ **deadly** [dédli]
- ☐ *put ~ back*
- ☐ **cage** [kéɪdʒ]
- ☐ **bite** [báɪt]

✤ KEY SENTENCES (☞ p. 91)

[75] I realized • that the danger was not • from the window • or the door, • but from the hole • in the wall.

[76] The bed was bolted • to the floor • so that • the rope could be used • as a bridge • for something • to pass through the wall • and come down to the bed.

"[77]The metallic noise Miss Stoner heard was the door of the safe closing as her father put the snake into its cage. Then I waited for the snake to come through the hole. When I heard its hiss, as I am sure you did, I lit the lamp and attacked it."

"So it turned back into the doctor's bedroom."

"And attacked him instead of us. [78]In this way, I am responsible for the man's death, but I cannot say that I am sad about it."

(85 [6,036] words)

ホームズは言った。「私に待ち伏せされたヘビは、医者の寝室に戻って代わりに彼を襲ったのだ。私は彼の死に責任があるが、悲しいとは言えない」

✤ KEYWORDS

- ☐ **noise** [nɔ́ɪz]
- ☐ **hiss** [hís]
- ☐ **attack** [ətǽk]
- ☐ **instead** [ìnstéd]
- ☐ *instead of*
- ☐ *in this way*
- ☐ **responsible** [rispɑ́ːnsəbəl]
- ☐ *be responsible for*
- ☐ **sad** [sǽd]

✤ KEY SENTENCES (☞ p. 91)

77 The metallic noise • Miss Stoner heard • was the door of the safe closing • as her father put the snake • into its cage.

78 In this way, • I am responsible for the man's death, • but I cannot say • that I am sad about it.

〈 KEY SENTENCES の訳 〉

1. "Ah, you have come at a perfect time, my dear Watson," Holmes said with a smile.
「ああ、ちょうどいい時に来てくれたね、親愛なるワトソン君」ホームズは笑顔で言った。

2. "I know that you are interested in my cases, because you have written so many of them into stories," said my friend.
「君が私の扱う事件に関心があるのは知ってるよ、なぜなら君はそれらの多くを物語で書いているからね」と私の友人は言った。

3. "Well, I think we have a case that will finally make you see things my way," said my friend with a smile.
「まあ、最終的には君に私の方法で物事を見させるような事件もあるだろう」と友人は笑顔で言った。

4. Usually, when I study a case, I think of thousands of other cases like it.
通常、私は事件を研究するとき、私は他の何千ものそれと同様なケースを考えます。

5. He believes in God, he has been to China, and recently he has done a lot of writing.
彼は神を信じ、中国に行ったことがあり、最近は多くの書きものをしている。

6. The bottom of your right sleeve is shiny because you have moved it along your writing paper as you sat at a desk writing, while the left elbow is thin where you rested it on the desk.
右袖の底の部分が光っているのは、机に座って書いているときに便箋に沿って袖を動かしていたからで、左肘は机の上に置いていた部分が薄くなっている。

7. I see a tattoo on your hand which could only have been painted in China.
中国でしか描くことができないタトゥーが手に入っているのが見えます。

8. No one will be impressed with me any more if I tell everything.
私がすべてを話してしまったら、もはや誰も私に感銘を受けないだろう。

9. I know he could make better money doing something else, but if he wants to work for me, I will not stop him.

彼が何か他のことをしてよりよいお金を稼ぐことができると知っていますが、もし彼が私のために働きたいと思うなら、私は彼を止めません。

10. I think he may be as unusual as the advertisement you have read us.
彼は、あなたが読んだ広告と同じくらい珍しいかもしれないと思いますよ。

11. Spaulding brought it to me saying, 'I wish I had red hair, Mr. Wilson.
スポールディングは「自分が赤髪だったらよかったのに、ウィルソンさん」とそれを私に持って来ました。

12. But you will be paid a couple hundred pounds a year extra.
しかし、あなたには年間数百ポンドが追加で支払われます。

13. I am sure that you would get the job if you went to the office next Monday, sir.
来週の月曜日に事務所に行ったら、あなたはきっと仕事に就くと思います。

14. Well, on that Monday at eleven o'clock, every man who had even a little red in his hair had come to the office of the League.
さて、その月曜日の11時に、髪の毛が少しでも赤い人は全員組合の事務所に来ていました。

15. Every red-headed man who came up to him, he asked a question and then sent him away.
彼のところにやって来た赤毛の男たち一人ひとりに、彼は質問をしてその後追い返していました。

16. Then he opened the door and shouted to the crowd that the job was taken.
それから彼はドアを開け、仕事の空きは埋まったと群衆に叫んだ。

17. This money was given to our organization so that more red-headed sons could be born.
このお金は、より多くの赤毛の息子が生まれるように、私たちの組織に与えられました。

18. Who would pay someone so much money for doing such easy work?
誰がそのような簡単な仕事をさせるためにそんなに多くのお金を払うだろうか？

19. At two o'clock, he said good-bye and was pleased that I had copied so many pages.
2時に、彼は別れを言って、私が非常に多くのページを写したことを喜びました。

20. Every morning I came in at ten and every afternoon I left at two.
私は毎朝10時に来て、毎日午後2時に出ました。

21. Sherlock Holmes and I both read the note again and then broke out laughing.
シャーロック・ホームズと私は二人とももう一度注意書きを読み、それからどっと笑い出した。

22. I went down to the ground floor and asked the owner of the building what had happened to the Red-headed League.
私は1階に降りて、ビルのオーナーに、赤毛組合に何が起こったのかを尋ねました。

23. How long had you known your assistant Spaulding before he found this advertisement?
彼がこの広告を見つける前に、どのくらいの間助手のスポールディングさんを知っていたのですか?

24. "Well, Watson," said Holmes when Mr. Wilson had gone, "what do you think?"
「さてワトソン」ホームズはウィルソン氏が出て行った時に言った。「どう思う?」

25. We took the subway to Aldersgate, then walked a short way to the small building that Mr. Wilson had told us about.
私たちは地下鉄でアルダーズゲートまで行き、ウィルソン氏が話した小さなビルまで近道を歩いて行った。

26. Then he walked up the street to the pawnshop and knocked at the door.
それから彼は通りを歩いて質屋に行き、ドアをノックした。

27. We turned the corner, we were on one of the most expensive streets in London.
私たちは角を曲がり、ロンドンで最も高級な通りの一つにいた。

28. Sometimes, it seemed that listening to music helped him solve his most difficult mysteries.
時には、音楽を聴くことが彼の最も困難な謎を解決するのに役立つようだった。

29. I did not understand what our business was that night.
私はその夜、私たちの仕事が何であるかを理解していなかった。

30. I couldn't understand anything, even though I had seen and heard every piece of evidence that Holmes had.
ホームズが持っていたすべての証拠を見聞きしたにもかかわらず、私は何も理解できなかった。

31. "I must ask you to be quiet, Mr. Merryweather."
「メリーウェザーさん、静かにしていただくようにお願いしなければなりません」

32. Watson, you must know that we are in the basement of one of the largest banks in London.
ワトソン、君は私たちがロンドンで最大の銀行の地下室にいることを知っている必要がある。

33. To me, it felt as though we waited the whole night, but I learned later that it was only a little more than an hour.
私には、一晩中待っていたかのように感じられたが、後でそれが1時間余りであることを知った。

34. Soon some stones were thrown aside and a young man's face looked into the room.
すぐにいくつかの石が脇に投げ出され、若い男の顔が部屋の中をのぞき込んだ。

35. "We've got you, and there are three men waiting for him at the door."
「我々はお前を捕まえた、そしてドアのところでは男が３人、奴を待ち構えている」

36. The criminals simply wanted to get Mr. Wilson out of the way for a few hours every day.
犯罪者たちは、ウィルソン氏を毎日数時間追い出したいと思っていただけだ。

37. When I heard the assistant was working for half pay, I thought he must have a reason.
助手が半額で働いていると聞いて、理由があるに違いないと思った。

38. When I heard that he spent hours in the basement, I thought he must be making a tunnel to another building.
彼が地下室で何時間も過ごしたと聞いたとき、私は彼が別の建物へのトンネルを作っているに違いないと思った。

39. They did not care if Mr. Wilson was in his store or not.
彼らはウィルソン氏が彼の店にいるかどうかは気にしなかった。

40. Saturday would be best because they had two days when the bank was closed.
土曜日は銀行が閉鎖されてから2日間あるので最良だった。

41. Early in April of 1883, I found Sherlock Holmes standing next to my bed waiting for me to wake up.
1883年4月の初め、私ははシャーロック・ホームズがベッドの隣に立って私が目を覚ますのを待っているのに気がついた。

42. When young ladies wake people early in the morning, there must be something very important to talk about.
若い女性が朝早くに人々を起こすときは、何かとても重要な話すことがあるに違いない。

43. She took off the veil and we could see that her face was pale, with frightened eyes.
彼女はベールを脱ぎ、私たちは彼女の顔が青白く、恐怖におびえた目をしているのを見ることができた。

44. I left home before six this morning and got the first train to Waterloo.
私は今朝6時前に家を出て、ウォータールー行きの最初の列車に乗りました。

45. Now, please give us the information that will make it possible to help you.
さて、私たちがお助けすることができるような情報をお願いします。

46. Even that one person who could help me thinks that my problems are in my own mind.
私を助けることができる一人でさえ、私の問題は私自身の心の中にあると思っています。

47. She gave him all of her money, with a note that some of the money would go to me and my sister when we were married.
彼女は、私たちが結婚するとき、お金の一部が私と私の妹に行くという遺書を残して、彼に彼女のお金のすべてを与えました。

48. When my mother died, he took us to live in his family house in the country.
私の母が死んだとき、彼は私たちを田舎の彼の一戸建ての家に住むために連れて行きました。

49. That is what I have come to talk to you about.

それが私があなたのところに来てお話ししたかったことです。

50. My sister went there at Christmas two years ago and met a nice man.
私の姉は2年前にクリスマスにそこに行き、素敵な男性に会いました。

51. But my sister could smell his cigars, which she didn't like, so she came into my room.
しかし、姉は、彼女が好きではない彼の葉巻の匂いがするため、私の部屋に入ってきました。

52. 'Tell me, Helen,' she said, 'have you ever heard anyone whistle late at night?'
「ヘレン、教えて」と彼女は言いました。「夜遅くに誰かが口笛を吹くのを聞いたことがある?」

53. I heard a whistle like she had described and then the sound of some metal falling.
私は彼女が説明したような笛の音と、なにか金属が落ちる音を聞きました。

54. "Well, I think I heard it but there was such a terrible storm, maybe it was in my head."
「さあ、私はそれを聞いたと思いますが、とてもひどい嵐でしたので、それは私の頭の中のことかもしれません」

55. "Of fear and nervous shock, but I don't know what frightened her."
「恐怖と神経性ショックのためだと、でも私は何が彼女を怖がらせたのか知りません」

56. "What do you think she meant by the 'speckled band'?"
「彼女の言う『まだらの紐』とはどういう意味だと思いますか?」

57. Imagine how frightened I was when I heard the whistle that she heard before her death.
彼女が死ぬ前に聞いた笛の音を聞いたとき、私がどれほど怖かったかを想像してみてください。

58. I got the train first thing this morning to visit you and ask for your advice.
あなたを訪ねて、アドバイスを伺おうと、今朝一番に列車に乗ったのです。

59. There are more details I wish to know.
もっと詳しく知りたいことがある。

60. "But I will return by the noon train to be there in time for your arrival."
「しかし、私はあなたの到着に間に合うように正午の列車で戻ります」

61. Just then a huge man with an evil face entered our room.
ちょうどその時、邪悪な顔をした大柄な男が私たちの部屋に入ってきた。

62. "Now we will have breakfast, Watson, and then I will go to the hospital where I will try to get some information before we take the train."
「さて、朝食を食べよう、ワトソン。それから私は列車に乗る前に何か情報を得るために病院に行ってこよう」

63. The income is now only 750 pounds a year, which means that in the case of marriage each daughter gets 250 pounds.
収入は現在、年間わずか750ポンドであり、結婚した場合、娘たちはそれぞれ250ポンドを得ることを意味する。

64. I would be very grateful if you would put your gun in your pocket.
君がポケットの中に銃を忍ばせてくれたら、とてもありがたい。

65. If he is angry with you tonight, we shall take you away to your aunt's at Harrow.
もし彼が今夜あなたに腹を立てているなら、私たちはあなたをハローの叔母の家に連れて行きます。

66. The building was old with broken windows covered with wooden boards.
建物は古く、壊れた窓は木の板で覆われていた。

67. There was a rope hanging over the bed for the servants' bell.
召使いの呼び鈴用にベッドの上にロープがぶら下がっていた。

68. There was also a hole in the ceiling connecting this room to the stepfather's bedroom.
天井には、この部屋と継父の寝室をつなぐ穴もあった。

69. Then he examined the chair carefully and noticed a dog leash tied to one corner of the bed.
それから彼は椅子を注意深く調べ、ベッドの片隅に結ばれた犬のリードに気づいた。

70. Then go to your room even though it is being torn up by the builders.
そして、建築業者に壊されているとしても、自分の部屋に行くように。

71. It is strange that after the rope and the hole in the ceiling are added to the room, the woman who sleeps there dies.
その部屋にロープと天井の穴が加わった後、そこで眠っていた女性が死んでしまうのは不思議なことである。

72. It was the lamp Holmes had told Miss Stoner to put there.
それは、ホームズがストーナー嬢に、そこに置くようにと言ったランプだった。

73. We found the safe open with Dr. Roylott sitting dead in the chair.
金庫が開いていて、ロイロット博士が椅子に座って死んでいるのを発見した。

74. He had a whistle in his hand and he was wearing a strange yellow band, with brown speckles, around his head.
手には笛を持っていて、頭には茶色の斑点が入った奇妙な黄色いバンドを巻いていた。

75. I realized that the danger was not from the window or the door, but from the hole in the wall.
危険なのは窓やドアではなく、壁の穴からだと気づいた。

76. The bed was bolted to the floor so that the rope could be used as a bridge for something to pass through the wall and come down to the bed.
ベッドは床にボルトで固定されていたので、ロープは何かが壁を通り抜けてベッドまで降りてくるための橋として使われていた。

77. The metallic noise Miss Stoner heard was the door of the safe closing as her father put the snake into its cage.
ストーナー嬢が聞いた金属音は、父親が蛇を檻に入れるときに金庫の扉が閉まる音だった。

78. In this way, I am responsible for the man's death, but I cannot say that I am sad about it.
このように、私は男の死には責任があるが、それを悲しんでいるとは言えない。

Word List

A B C D E F G H I J K L M N O P Q R S T U V W X Y Z

・語形が規則変化する語の見出しは原形で示しています。不規則変化語は本文中で使われている形になっています。
・一般的な意味を紹介していますので、一部の語で本文で実際に使われている品詞や意味と合っていないことがあります。
・品詞は以下のように示しています。

名 名詞	代 代名詞	形 形容詞	副 副詞	動 動詞	助 助動詞
前 前置詞	接 接続詞	間 間投詞	冠 冠詞	略 略語	俗 俗語
熟 熟語	頭 接頭語	尾 接尾語	号 記号	関 関係代名詞	

A

□ **a** 冠 ①1つの，1人の，ある ②～につき

□ **able** 形 ①《be – to ～》(人が)～することができる ②能力のある

□ **about** 副 ①およそ，約 ②まわりに，あたりを 前 ①～について ②～のまわりに[の] **How about ～?** ～はどうですか。～しませんか。 **What about ～?** ～についてあなたはどう思いますか。～はどうですか。 **sure about**《be –》～に確信を持っている **talk to someone about** ～のことで(人)に話しかける **worry about** ～のことを心配する

□ **above** 前 ①～の上に ②～より上で，～以上で ③～を超えて 副 ①上に ②以上に 形 上記の 名《the –》上記の人[こと]

□ **accident** 名 ①(不慮の)事故，災難 ②偶然

□ **across** 前 ～を渡って，～の向こう側に，(身体の一部に)かけて 副 渡って，向こう側に **go across** 横断する，渡る

□ **act** 名 行為，行い 動 ①行動する ②機能する ③演じる

□ **add** 動 ①加える，足す ②足し算をする ③言い添える

□ **adder** 名 クサリヘビ，アダー《クサリヘビ科の毒ヘビ》 **swamp adder** 沼の毒ヘビ

□ **address** 名 ①住所，アドレス ②演説 動 ①あて名を書く ②演説をする，話しかける

□ **adventure** 名 冒険 動 危険をおかす

□ **advertisement** 名 広告，宣伝

□ **advice** 名 忠告，助言，意見

□ **affect** 動 ①影響する ②(病気などが)おかす ③ふりをする 名 感情，欲望

□ **afraid** 形 ①心配して ②恐れて，こわがって **afraid of**《be –》～を

恐れる, ～を怖がる

□ **after** 前 ①～の後に[で], ～の次に ②《前後に名詞がきて》次々に～, 何度も～《反復・継続を表す》 副 後に[で] 接 (～した) 後に[で] 動 ～の後を追って, ～を捜して

□ **afternoon** 名 午後

□ **again** 副 再び, もう一度

□ **against** 前 ①～に対して, ～に反対して, (規則など) に違反して ②～にもたれて

□ **ago** 副 ～前に

□ **ah** 間《驚き・悲しみ・賞賛などを表して》ああ, やっぱり

□ **Aldersgate** 名 アルダーズゲート《かつてロンドンを囲んでいた「ロンドン・ウォール」にあった門。現在はその名を冠した区および通りがある》

□ **all** 形 すべての, ～中 代 全部, すべて (のもの[人]) 名 全体 副 まったく, すっかり **all around** 辺り一帯に, 至る所に **all day** 一日中, 明けても暮れても **all over** すっかり[全て]終わって **all right** 大丈夫で, よろしい, わかった **Not at all.** 全くそんなことはありません。どういたしまして。 **not ～ at all** 全く～でない **That is all for now.** 今のところ以上です。

□ **allow** 動 ①許す, 《－ … to ～》…が～するのを可能にする, …に～させておく ②与える

□ **almost** 副 ほとんど, もう少しで (～するところ)

□ **alone** 形 ただひとりの 副 ひとりで, ～だけで

□ **along** 前 ～に沿って 副 ～に沿って, 前へ, 進んで **come along** 一緒に来る, ついて来る **move along** ～に沿って動く

□ **already** 副 すでに, もう

□ **also** 副 ～も(また), ～も同様に 接 その上, さらに

□ **always** 副 いつも, 常に

□ **am** 動 ～である, (～に) いる[ある]《主語がIのときのbeの現在形》

□ **American** 形 アメリカ(人)の 名 アメリカ人

□ **an** 冠 ①1つの, 1人の, ある ②～につき

□ **and** 接 ①そして, ～と… ②《同じ語を結んで》ますます ③《結果を表して》それで, だから

□ **angry** 形 怒って, 腹を立てて

□ **animal** 名 動物 形 動物の

□ **another** 形 ①もう1つ[1人]の ②別の 代 ①もう1つ[1人] ②別のもの

□ **answer** 動 ①答える, 応じる ②《－ for ～》～の責任を負う 名 答え, 応答, 返事

□ **any** 形 ①《疑問文で》何か, いくつかの ②《否定文で》何も, 少しも(～ない) ③《肯定文で》どの～も **any longer** これ以上, もっと長く 代 ①《疑問文で》(～のうち) 何か, どれか, 誰か ②《否定文で》少しも, 何も[誰も] ～ない ③《肯定文で》どれも, 誰でも

□ **anybody** 代 ①《疑問文・条件節で》誰か ②《否定文で》誰も(～ない) ③《肯定文で》誰でも **anybody who** ～する人はだれでも

□ **anyone** 代 ①《疑問文·条件節で》誰か ②《否定文で》誰も(～ない) ③《肯定文で》誰でも

□ **anything** 代 ①《疑問文で》何か, どれでも ②《否定文で》何も, どれも(～ない) ③《肯定文で》何でも, どれでも 副 いくらか

□ **anyway** 副 ①いずれにせよ, ともかく ②どんな方法でも

□ **apply** 動 ①申し込む, 志願する ②あてはまる ③適用する

□ **April** 名 4月

□ **Archie** 名 アーチー《人名》

□ **are** 動 ～である, (～に)いる[ある]《主語がyou, we, theyまたは複数名詞のときのbeの現在形》

□ **arm** 名 ①腕 ②腕状のもの, 腕木, ひじかけ **hold someone in one's arms** (人)を抱き締める

□ **around** 副 ①まわりに, あちこちに ②およそ, 約 前 ～のまわりに, ～のあちこちに **all around** 辺り一帯に, 至る所に **walk around** 歩き回る, ぶらぶら歩く

□ **arrival** 名 ①到着 ②到達

□ **arrive** 動 到着する, 到達する **arrive at** ～に着く

□ **as** 接 ①《as ～ as …の形で》…と同じくらい～ ②～のとおりに, ～のように ③～しながら, ～しているときに ④～するにつれて, ～にしたがって ⑤～なので ⑥～だけれども ⑦～する限りでは 前 ①～として(の) ②～の時 副 同じくらい 代 ①～のような ②～だが **as soon as possible** できるだけ早く, 速やかに **as though** あたかも～のように, まるで～みたいに **as usual** いつものように, 相変わらず **as well** 同様に, その上

□ **aside** 副 わきへ(に), 離れて **throw aside** わきに投げ捨てる

□ **ask** 動 ①尋ねる, 聞く ②頼む, 求める

□ **asleep** 形 眠って(いる状態の) 副 眠って, 休止して **fall asleep** 眠り込む, 寝入る

□ **assistant** 名 助手, 補佐, 店員 形 援助の, 補佐の

□ **at** 前 ①《場所·時》～に[で] ②《目標·方向》～に[を], ～に向かって ③《原因·理由》～を見て[聞いて·知って] ④～に従事して, ～の状態で

□ **attack** 動 ①襲う, 攻める ②非難する ③(病気が)おかす 名 ①攻撃, 非難 ②発作, 発病

□ **aunt** 名 おば

□ **away** 副 離れて, 遠くに, 去って, わきに **send ～ away** ～を追い払う, 送り出す **take someone away** (人)を連れ出す 形 離れた, 遠征した

B

□ **back** 名 ①背中 ②裏, 後ろ 副 ①戻って ②後ろへ[に] 形 裏の, 後ろの 動 後ろへ動く, 後退する **come back** 戻る **push back** 押し返す, 押しのける **put ～ back** ～を(もとの場所に)戻す, 返す **turn back** 元に戻る

□ **bad** 形 ①悪い, へたな, まずい ②気の毒な ③(程度が)ひどい, 激しい

□ **badly** 副 ①悪く，まずく，へたに ②とても，ひどく

□ **bag** 名 袋，かばん 動 袋に入れる，つかまえる

□ **band** 名 ①ひも，帯 ②楽団，団（party） ③縞模様 動 ①ひもで縛る ②団結する［させる］

□ **bank** 名 ①銀行 ②堤防，岸 動 ①（銀行と）取引する ②積み上げる

□ **basement** 名 地下（室），基部

□ **be** 動 ～である，（～に）いる［ある］，～となる 助 ①《現在分詞とともに用いて》～している ②《過去分詞とともに用いて》～される，～されている

□ **beat** 動 ①打つ，鼓動する ②打ち負かす 名 打つこと，鼓動，拍

□ **became** 動 become（なる）の過去

□ **because** 接（なぜなら）～だから，～という理由［原因］で

□ **bed** 名 ①ベッド，寝所 ②花壇，川床，土台 **go to bed** 床につく，寝る

□ **bedclothes** 名 寝具

□ **bedroom** 名 寝室

□ **been** 動 be（～である）の過去分詞 助 be（～している・～される）の過去分詞 **have been to** ～へ行ったことがある

□ **before** 前 ～の前に［で］，～より以前に 接 ～する前に 副 以前に

□ **began** 動 begin（始まる）の過去

□ **begin** 動 始まる［始める］，起こる

□ **behind** 前 ①～の後ろに，～の背後に ②～に遅れて，～に劣って **close ～ behind …** …を～の後ろで閉める 副 ①後ろに，背後に ②遅れて，劣って

□ **being** 動 be（～である）の現在分詞 名 存在，生命，人間

□ **believe** 動 信じる，信じている，（～と）思う，考える **believe in** ～を信じる

□ **bell** 名 ベル，鈴，鐘 動 ①（ベル・鐘が）鳴る ②ベル［鈴］をつける

□ **bent** 動 bend（曲がる）の過去，過去分詞 形 ①曲がった ②熱中した，決心した 名（生まれつきの）好み，傾向

□ **beside** 前 ①～のそばに，～と並んで ②～と比べると ③～とはずれて

□ **best** 形 最もよい，最大［多］の 副 最もよく，最も上手に 名《the –》①最上のもの ②全力，精いっぱい

□ **better** 形 ①よりよい ②（人が）回復して 副 ①よりよく，より上手に ②むしろ **better not** ～しない方がよい **feel better** 気分がよくなる

□ **between** 前（2つのもの）の間に［で・の］ 副 間に

□ **big** 形 ①大きい ②偉い，重要な 副 ①大きく，大いに ②自慢して

□ **bite** 動 かむ，かじる 名 かむこと，かみ傷，ひと口

□ **black** 形 黒い，有色の 名 黒，黒色 **dressed in black** 黒ずくめの服装をしている

□ **blazing** 形 ①赤々と燃え上がる

②非常に魅力的な ③炎暑の，非常に暑い

□ **blue** 形 ①青い ②青ざめた ③憂うつな，陰気な 名 青(色)

□ **board** 名 ①板，掲示板 ②委員会，重役会 動 ①乗り込む ②下宿する

□ **body** 名 ①体，死体，胴体 ②団体，組織 ③主要部，(文書の)本文

□ **bolt** 名 ①ボルト ②かんぬき ③稲妻 動 かんぬきをかける

□ **book** 名 ①本，書物 ②《the B-》聖書 ③《-s》帳簿 動 ①記入する，記帳する ②予約する

□ **boredom** 名 退屈

□ **born** 動 **be born** 生まれる 形 生まれた，生まれながらの

□ **both** 形 両方の，2つともの 副《both ～ and … の形で》～も…も両方とも 代 両方，両者，双方

□ **bottle** 名 瓶，ボトル 動 瓶に入れる[詰める]

□ **bottom** 名 ①底，下部，すそ野，ふもと，最下位，根底 ②尻 形 底の，根底の

□ **bought** 動 buy (買う) の過去，過去分詞

□ **box** 名 ①箱，容器 ②観覧席 ③詰所 動 ①箱に入れる[詰める] ②ボクシングをする

□ **brave** 形 勇敢な 動 勇敢に立ち向かう

□ **break in** 会話に入り込む，話に割り込む

□ **break out laughing** どっと笑い出す

□ **breakfast** 名 朝食

□ **brick** 名 レンガ，レンガ状のもの 形 レンガ造りの

□ **bridge** 名 橋 動 橋をかける

□ **bright** 形 ①輝いている，鮮明な ②快活な ③利口な 副 輝いて，明るく

□ **bring** 動 ①持ってくる，連れてくる ②もたらす，生じる

□ **broke** 動 break (壊す) の過去

□ **broken** 動 break (壊す) の過去分詞 形 ①破れた，壊れた ②落胆した

□ **brought** 動 bring (持ってくる) の過去，過去分詞

□ **brown** 形 ①茶色の ②浅黒い肌の，日焼けした 名 ①茶色(のもの) ②浅黒い肌の人 動 茶色にする，日焼けする[させる]

□ **bruise** 動 ①(人や果物に)傷をつける ②(感情などを)傷つける 名 打撲傷

□ **builder** 名 建設者

□ **building** 動 build (建てる) の現在分詞 名 建物，建造物，ビルディング

□ **business** 名 ①職業，仕事 ②商売 ③用事 ④出来事，やっかいなこと 形 ①職業の ②商売上の

□ **busy** 形 ①忙しい ②(電話で)話し中で ③にぎやかな，交通が激しい

□ **but** 接 ①でも，しかし ②～を除いて **not ～ but** … ～ではなくて… 前 ～を除いて，～のほかは 副 ただ，のみ，ほんの

□ **by** 前 ①《位置》～のそばに[で] ②《手段・方法・行為者・基準》

～によって，～で ③《期限》～までには ④《通過・経由》～を経由して，～を通って **mean A by B** Aという意味でBと言う 副 そばに，通り過ぎて

C

- □ **cab** 名 タクシー
- □ **cage** 名 鳥かご，檻
- □ **call** 動 ①呼ぶ，叫ぶ ②電話をかける ③立ち寄る 名 ①呼び声，叫び ②電話（をかけること） ③短い訪問
- □ **came** 動 come（来る）の過去
- □ **can** 助 ①～できる ②～してもよい ③～でありうる ④《否定文で》～のはずがない **Can you ～?** ～してくれますか。
- □ **cane** 名 ①茎 ②（籐製の）杖
- □ **car** 名 自動車，（列車の）車両
- □ **card** 名 ①カード，券，名刺，はがき ②トランプ，《-s》トランプ遊び **play cards** トランプ［で賭け］をする
- □ **care** 名 ①心配，注意 ②世話，介護 **take care of** ～の面倒を見る，～を管理する 動 ①《通例否定文・疑問文で》気にする，心配する ②世話をする
- □ **careful** 形 注意深い，慎重な
- □ **carefully** 副 注意深く，丹念に
- □ **carpet** 名 じゅうたん，敷物
- □ **case** 名 ①事件，問題，事柄 ②実例，場合 ③実状，状況，症状 ④箱 **in the case of** ～の場合は
- □ **cat** 名 ネコ（猫）
- □ **caught** 動 catch（つかまえる）の過去，過去分詞
- □ **cause** 名 ①原因，理由，動機 ②大義，主張 動（～の）原因となる，引き起こす
- □ **ceiling** 名 ①天井 ②上限，最高価格
- □ **chain** 名 ①鎖 ②一続き 動 ①鎖でつなぐ ②束縛［拘束］する
- □ **chair** 名 ①いす ②《the –》議長［会長］の席［職］
- □ **change** 動 ①変わる，変える ②交換する ③両替する
- □ **check** 動 ①照合する，検査する ②阻止［妨害］する ③（所持品を）預ける
- □ **chief** 名 頭，長，親分 形 最高位の，第一の，主要な
- □ **China** 名 ①中国《国名》 ②《c-》陶磁器，瀬戸物
- □ **Christmas** 名 クリスマス
- □ **cigar** 名 葉巻
- □ **clay** 名 粘土，白土
- □ **clean** 形 ①きれいな，清潔な ②正当な 動 掃除する，よごれを落とす 副 ①きれいに ②まったく，すっかり
- □ **clear** 形 ①はっきりした，明白な ②澄んだ ③（よく）晴れた 動 ①はっきりさせる ②片づける ③晴れる 副 ①はっきりと ②すっかり，完全に
- □ **clever** 形 ①頭のよい，利口な ②器用な，上手な
- □ **climb** 動 登る，徐々に上がる 名 登ること，上昇

□ **close** 形 ①近い ②親しい ③狭い 副 ①接近して ②密集して 動 ①閉まる, 閉める ②終える, 閉店する **close ~ behind** … …を~の後ろで閉める

□ **closed** 動 close (閉まる) の過去, 過去分詞 形 閉じた, 閉鎖した

□ **cloth** 名 布 (地), テーブルクロス, ふきん

□ **clothes** 動 clothe (服を着せる) の3人称単数現在 名 衣服, 身につけるもの

□ **club** 名 ①クラブ, (同好) 会 ②こん棒 動 こん棒で打つ [なぐる]

□ **coat** 名 ①コート ② (動物の) 毛 動 ①表面を覆う ②上着を着せる

□ **coin** 名 硬貨, コイン 動 (硬貨を) 鋳造する

□ **cold** 形 ①寒い, 冷たい ②冷淡な, 冷静な 名 ①寒さ, 冷たさ ②風邪

□ **color** 名 ①色, 色彩 ②絵の具 ③血色 動 色をつける

□ **come** 動 ①来る, 行く, 現れる ② (出来事が) 起こる, 生じる ③~になる ④comeの過去分詞 **come along** 一緒に来る, ついて来る **come back** 戻る **come down to** ~へ下りて来る, ~まで下げる **come for** ~の目的で来る, ~を取りに来る **come in** 中にはいる, やってくる, 出回る **come into** ~に入ってくる **come out of** ①~から出てくる ②~から採れる, 産出される **come running from** ~から飛んでくる, かけつける **come through** 通り抜ける **come to an end** 終わる **come up to** ~までやってくる, 近づいてくる

□ **comfortably** 副 心地よく, くつろいで

□ **company** 名 ①会社 ②交際, 同席 ③友だち, 仲間, 一団, 人の集まり **enjoy each other's company** お互いに楽しくやる

□ **completely** 副 完全に, すっかり

□ **compliment** 名 ①賛辞, 敬意 ②《-s》あいさつ 動 ほめる, お世辞を言う

□ **concert** 名 ①音楽 [演奏] 会, コンサート ②一致, 協力

□ **congratulate** 動 祝う, 祝辞を述べる

□ **congratulation** 間《-s》おめでとう 名 祝賀, 祝い,《-s》祝いの言葉

□ **connect** 動 つながる, つなぐ, 関係づける

□ **continue** 動 続く, 続ける, (中断後) 再開する, (ある方向に) 移動していく

□ **conversation** 名 会話, 会談

□ **cook** 動 料理する, (食物が) 煮える 名 料理人, コック

□ **copy** 名 ①コピー, 写し ② (書籍の) 一部, 冊 ③広告文 動 写す, まねる, コピーする

□ **corner** 名 ①曲がり角, 角 ②すみ, はずれ 動 ①窮地に追いやる ②買い占める ③角を曲がる

□ **coroner** 名 検死官

□ **could** 助 ①can (~できる) の過去 ②《控え目な推量・可能性・願望などを表す》 **How could ~?** 何だって~なんてことがありえようか?

□ **country** 名 ①国 ②《the –》田舎, 郊外 ③地域, 領域, 分野 形 田舎の, 野暮な

□ **couple** 名 ①2つ, 対 ②夫婦, 一組 ③数個 動 つなぐ, つながる, 関連させる

□ **course** 名 ①進路, 方向 ②経過, 成り行き ③科目, 講座 ④策 , 方策 **of course** もちろん, 当然

□ **cover** 動 ①覆う, 包む, 隠す ②扱う, (〜に) わたる, 及ぶ ③代わりを務める ④補う 名 覆い, カバー

□ **crack** 名 ①割れ目, ひび ②(裂けるような) 鋭い音 動 ①ひびが入る, ひびを入れる, 割れる, 割る ②鈍い音を出す

□ **crime** 名 ①(法律上の) 罪, 犯罪 ②悪事, よくない行為

□ **criminal** 形 犯罪の, 罪深い, 恥ずべき 名 犯罪者, 犯人

□ **cross** 動 ①横切る, 渡る ②じゃまする ③十字を切る 名 十字架, 十字形のもの 形 不機嫌な

□ **crowd** 動 群がる, 混雑する 名 群集, 雑踏, 多数, 聴衆

□ **cruelly** 副 残酷に

□ **cry** 動 泣く, 叫ぶ, 大声を出す, 嘆く **cry out** 叫ぶ 名 泣き声, 叫び, かっさい

□ **curl** 名 巻き毛, 渦巻状のもの 動 カールする, 巻きつく

D

□ **danger** 名 危険, 障害, 脅威 **walk through the dangers** 危険を乗り越える

□ **dangerous** 形 危険な, 有害な

□ **dark** 形 ①暗い, 闇の ②(色が) 濃い, (髪が) 黒い ③陰うつな 名 ①《the –》暗がり, 闇 ②日暮れ, 夜 ③暗い色[影]

□ **date** 名 ①日付, 年月日 ②デート 動 ①日付を記す ②デートする

□ **daughter** 名 娘

□ **day** 名 ①日中, 昼間 ②日, 期日 ③《-s》時代, 生涯 **all day** 一日中, 明けても暮れても **day off work**《a –》〔平日に取る〕休日 **every day** 毎日 **one day** (過去の) ある日, (未来の) いつか

□ **dead** 形 ①死んでいる, 活気のない, 枯れた ②まったくの 名《the –》死者たち, 故人 副 完全に, まったく

□ **deadliest** 形 deadly (致命的な) の最上級

□ **deadly** 形 命にかかわる, 痛烈な, 破壊的な 副 ひどく, 極度に

□ **dear** 形 いとしい, 親愛なる, 大事な 名 ねえ, あなた《呼びかけ》 間 まあ, おや **Dear me!** おや！, まあ！《驚きを表す》

□ **death** 名 ①死, 死ぬこと ②《the –》終えん, 消滅

□ **decide to do** 〜することに決める

□ **decided** 動 decide (決定する) の過去, 過去分詞 形 はっきりした, 断固とした

□ **deep** 形 ①深い, 深さ〜の ②深遠な ③濃い 副 深く

□ **demand** 動 ①要求する, 尋ねる ②必要とする 名 ①要求, 請求

②需要

□ **depend** 動《– on [upon] ～》①～を頼る，～をあてにする ②～による，～しだいである

□ **describe** 動（言葉で）描写する，特色を述べる，説明する

□ **desk** 名 ①机，台 ②受付（係），フロント，カウンター，部局

□ **detail** 名 ①細部，《-s》詳細 ②《-s》個人情報 動 詳しく述べる

□ **develop** 動 ①発達する［させる］ ②開発する

□ **did** 動 do（～をする）の過去 助 doの過去

□ **die** 動 死ぬ，消滅する **die of** ～がもとで死ぬ

□ **different** 形 異なった，違った，別の，さまざまな **different from**《be –》～と違う

□ **difficult** 形 困難な，むずかしい，扱いにくい

□ **digging** 名 ①掘ること，採掘 ②《-s》採掘現場 ③《-s》下宿，居所

□ **director** 名 管理者，指導者，監督

□ **disagree** 動 異議を唱える，反対する

□ **discourage** 動 ①やる気をそぐ，失望させる ②（～するのを）阻止する，やめさせる

□ **dish** 名 ①大皿 ②料理

□ **dissolve** 動 ①溶ける，溶かす ②消える，解散する ③解決する

□ **do** 助 ①《ほかの動詞とともに用いて現在形の否定文・疑問文をつくる》②《同じ動詞を繰り返す代わりに用いる》③《動詞を強調するのに用いる》 動 ～をする

□ **doctor** 名 医者，博士（号）

□ **does** 動 do（～をする）の3人称単数現在 助 doの3人称単数現在

□ **dog** 名 犬

□ **doing** 動 do（～をする）の現在分詞 **start doing** ～し始める 名 ①すること，したこと ②《-s》行為，出来事

□ **done** 動 do（～をする）の過去分詞

□ **door** 名 ①ドア，戸 ②一軒，一戸

□ **down** 副 ①下へ，降りて，低くなって ②倒れて 前 ～の下方へ，～を下って 形 下方の，下りの **come down to** ～へ下りて来る，～まで下げる **get down** 降りる，着地する，身をかがめる **go down** 下に降りる **lead someone down**（人）を～に案内する［連れて行く］ **run down** 駆け下りる **throw oneself down on** ～に身を投げ出す，寝転がる **walk up and down** 行ったり来たりする

□ **downstairs** 副 階下で，下の部屋で 形 階下の 名 階下

□ **Dr. Roylott** ロイロット博士《人名》

□ **dress** 名 ドレス，衣服，正装 動 ①服を着る［着せる］ ②飾る **dressed in black** 黒ずくめの服装をしている

□ **dressing** 動 dress（服を着る）の現在分詞 名 ①ドレッシング ②着付け，衣装 ③手当て，手入れ，下ごしらえ

☐ **dressing-table** 名 化粧台, 鏡台

☐ **drive** 動 ①車で行く, (車を) 運転する ②追いやる, (ある状態に) する 名 ドライブ

☐ **driver** 名 ①運転手 ②(馬車の) 御者

☐ **drop** 動 ①(ぽたぽた) 落ちる, 落とす ②下がる, 下げる 名 しずく, 落下

☐ **Duncan Ross** ダンカン・ロス《人名》

☐ **during** 前 ～の間 (ずっと)

E

☐ **each** 形 それぞれの, 各自の **enjoy each other's company** お互いに楽しくやる 代 それぞれ, 各自 副 それぞれに

☐ **ear** 名 耳, 聴覚

☐ **early** 形 ①(時間や時期が) 早い ②初期の, 幼少の, 若い 副 ①早く, 早めに ②初期に, 初めのころに

☐ **earring** 名《通例 -s》イヤリング

☐ **easily** 副 ①容易に, たやすく, 苦もなく ②気楽に

☐ **easy** 形 ①やさしい, 簡単な ②気楽な, くつろいだ

☐ **eight** 名 8 (の数字), 8人 [個] 形 8の, 8人 [個] の

☐ **elbow** 名 ひじ 動 ひじで突く [押す], 押し分けて進む

☐ **eleven** 名 ①11 (の数字), 11人 [個] ②11人のチーム, イレブン 形 11の, 11人 [個] の

☐ **else** 副 ①そのほかに [の], 代わりに ②さもないと

☐ **embarrassed** 動 embarrass (恥ずかしい思いをさせる) の過去, 過去分詞 形 恥ずかしい, 当惑して

☐ **empty** 形 ①空の, 空いている ②(心などが) ぼんやりした, 無意味な 動 空になる [する], 注ぐ

☐ **encyclopedia** 名 百科事典

☐ **Encyclopedia Britannica** 《商標》ブリタニカ百科事典

☐ **end** 名 ①終わり, 終末, 死 ②果て, 末, 端 ③目的 **come to an end** 終わる 動 終わる, 終える

☐ **enemy** 名 敵

☐ **engaged** 動 engage (約束する) の過去, 過去分詞 形 ①婚約した ②忙しい, ふさがっている

☐ **England** 名 ①イングランド ②英国

☐ **enjoy** 動 楽しむ, 享受する **enjoy each other's company** お互いに楽しくやる

☐ **enough** 形 十分な, (～するに) 足る 代 十分 (な量・数), たくさん 副 (～できる) だけ, 十分に, まったく

☐ **enter** 動 ①入る, 入会 [入学] する [させる] ②記入する ③(考えなどが) (心・頭に) 浮かぶ

☐ **escape** 動 逃げる, 免れる, もれる 名 逃亡, 脱出, もれ **way of escape** 逃げ道

☐ **even** 副 ①《強意》～でさえも, ～ですら, いっそう, なおさら ②平等に **even that** それすら **even though** ～であるけれども, ～にもかかわらず 形 ①平らな, 水平の ②等しい, 均一の ③落ち着いた

動平らになる[する], 釣り合いがとれる

□ **evening** 名 ①夕方, 晩 ②《the [one's] –》末期, 晩年, 衰退期

□ **event** 名出来事, 事件, イベント

□ **ever** 副 ①今までに, これまで, かつて, いつまでも ②《強意》いったい

□ **every** 形 ①どの～も, すべての, あらゆる ②毎～, ～ごとの **every day** 毎日

□ **everyday** 形毎日の, 日々の

□ **everyone** 代誰でも, 皆

□ **everything** 代すべてのこと[もの], 何でも, 何もかも

□ **evidence** 名 ①証拠, 証人 ②形跡

□ **evil** 形 ①邪悪な ②有害な, 不吉な 名 ①邪悪 ②害, わざわい, 不幸 副悪く

□ **exactly** 副 ①正確に, 厳密に, ちょうど ②まったくそのとおり

□ **examine** 動試験する, 調査[検査]する, 診察する

□ **except** 前 ～を除いて, ～のほかは 接 ～ということを除いて

□ **exciting** 動excite (興奮する) の現在分詞 形興奮させる, わくわくさせる

□ **excuse** 動 ①(～の) 言い訳をする ②許す, 容赦する, 免除する 名 ①言い訳, 口実 ②免除

□ **expect** 動予期[予測]する, (当然のこととして) 期待する

□ **expensive** 形高価な, ぜいたくな

□ **explain** 動説明する, 明らかにする, 釈明[弁明]する

□ **extra** 形余分の, 臨時の 名 ①余分なもの ②エキストラ 副余分に

□ **eye** 名 ①目, 視力 ②眼識, 観察力 ③注目

F

□ **face** 名 ①顔, 顔つき ②外観, 外見 ③(時計の) 文字盤, (建物の) 正面 動直面する, 立ち向かう

□ **fall** 動 ①落ちる, 倒れる ②(値段・温度が) 下がる ③(ある状態に) 急に陥る **fall asleep** 眠り込む, 寝入る **fall to the ground** 転ぶ 名 ①落下, 墜落 ②滝 ③崩壊 ④秋

□ **family** 名家族, 家庭, 一門, 家柄

□ **fast** 形 ①(速度が) 速い ②(時計が) 進んでいる ③しっかりした 副 ①速く, 急いで ②(時計が) 進んで ③しっかりと, ぐっすりと

□ **father** 名 ①父親 ②先祖, 創始者 ③《F-》神 ④神父, 司祭

□ **fear** 名 ①恐れ ②心配, 不安 動 ①恐れる ②心配する

□ **feel** 動感じる, (～と) 思う **feel better** 気分がよくなる

□ **fell** 動fall (落ちる) の過去

□ **felt** 動feel (感じる) の過去, 過去分詞 名フェルト 形フェルト(製)の

□ **few** 形 ①ほとんどない, 少数の(～しかない) ②《a –》少数の, 少しはある 代少数の人[物]

□ **field** 名 ①野原, 田畑, 広がり ②(研究) 分野 ③競技場

□ **fight with** ～と戦う

□ **figure** 名 ①人[物]の姿, 形 ②図(形) ③数字 動 ①描写する, 想像する ②計算する ③目立つ, (～として)現れる **figure out** 理解する, (原因などを)解明する, 見当がつく

□ **fill** 動 ①満ちる, 満たす ②《be -ed with ～》～でいっぱいである

□ **finally** 副 最後に, ついに, 結局

□ **find** 動 ①見つける ②(～と)わかる, 気づく, ～と考える ③得る

□ **fine** 形 ①元気な ②美しい, りっぱな, 申し分ない, 結構な ③晴れた ④細かい, 微妙な **fine man** 立派な男性 副 りっぱに, 申し分なく

□ **finished** 動 finish(終わる)の過去, 過去分詞 形 ①終わった, 仕上がった ②洗練された ③もうだめになった

□ **fire** 名 ①火, 炎, 火事 ②砲火, 攻撃 **open fire** 発砲を開始する 動 ①発射する ②解雇する ③火をつける

□ **first** 名 最初, 第一(の人・物) 形 ①第一の, 最初の ②最も重要な 副 第一に, 最初に **at first** 最初は, 初めのうちは **first thing** 真っ先に

□ **fix** 動 ①固定する[させる] ②修理する ③決定する ④用意する, 整える

□ **Fleet Street** フリート・ストリート《ロンドンにある通り》

□ **floor** 名 床, 階 **ground floor** 1階

□ **follow** 動 ①ついていく, あとをたどる ②(～の)結果として起こる ③(忠告などに)従う ④理解できる

□ **following** 動 follow(ついていく)の現在分詞 形《the –》次の, 次に続く 名《the –》下記のもの, 以下に述べるもの

□ **for** 前 ①《目的・原因・対象》～にとって, ～のために[の], ～に対して ②《期間》～間 ③《代理》～の代わりに ④《方向》～へ(向かって) 接 というわけは～, なぜなら～, だから

□ **forever** 副 永遠に, 絶えず

□ **fought** 動 fight(戦う)の過去, 過去分詞

□ **found** 動 ①find(見つける)の過去, 過去分詞 ②～の基礎を築く, ～を設立する

□ **four** 名 4(の数字), 4人[個] 形 4の, 4人[個]の

□ **fourteen** 名 14(の数字), 14人[個] 形 14の, 14人[個]の

□ **fourth** 名 第4番目(の人・物), 4日 形 第4番目の

□ **fourth-smartest** 形 4番目に賢い

□ **France** 名 フランス《国名》

□ **French** 形 フランス(人・語)の 名 ①フランス語 ②《the –》フランス人

□ **Friday** 名 金曜日

□ **friend** 名 友だち, 仲間

□ **friendly** 形 親しみのある, 親切な, 友情のこもった 副 友好的に, 親切に

□ **frighten** 動〔人を〕怖がらせる[怖がる], ぎくりとさせる[する]

□ **frightened** 動 frighten(驚かせる)の過去, 過去分詞 形 おびえた, びっくりした

□ **from** 前 ①《出身・出発点・時間・順序・原料》～から ②《原因・理由》～がもとで **from time to time** ときどき **from ～ to …** ～から…まで

□ **front** 名正面, 前 形正面の, 前面の

□ **full** 形 ①満ちた, いっぱいの, 満期の ②完全な, 盛りの, 充実した **full of**《be －》～で一杯である 名全部

□ **funny** 形 ①おもしろい, こっけいな ②奇妙な, うさんくさい

G

□ **game** 名ゲーム, 試合, 遊び, 競技 動賭けごとをする

□ **gave** 動give（与える）の過去

□ **gentlemen** 名gentleman（紳士）の複数

□ **get** 動 ①得る, 手に入れる ②（ある状態に）なる, いたる ③わかる, 理解する ④～させる, ～を（…の状態に）する ⑤（ある場所に）達する, 着く **get down** 降りる, 着地する, 身をかがめる **get out of** ～から下車する **get someone to do**（人）に～させる［してもらう］ **get up** 起き上がる, 立ち上がる **get ～ out of the way** ～を追い出す, どかす

□ **girl** 名女の子, 少女

□ **give** 動 ①与える, 贈る ②伝える, 述べる ③（～を）する **give up** あきらめる, やめる, 引き渡す

□ **given** 動give（与える）の過去分詞 形与えられた

□ **glad** 形 ①うれしい, 喜ばしい ②《be － to ～》～してうれしい, 喜んで～する

□ **glove** 名手袋, グローブ

□ **go** 動 ①行く, 出かける ②動く ③進む, 経過する, いたる ④（ある状態に）なる **be going to** ～するつもりである **go across** 横断する, 渡る **go down** 下に降りる **go home** 帰宅する **go into** ～に入る **go over to** ～の前に［へ］行く, ～に出向いて行く **go to bed** 床につく, 寝る

□ **god** 名神

□ **gold** 名金, 金貨, 金製品, 金色 形金の, 金製の, 金色の

□ **gone** 動go（行く）の過去分詞 形去った, 使い果たした, 死んだ

□ **good** 形 ①よい, 上手な, 優れた, 美しい ②（数量・程度が）かなりの, 相当な 間よかった, わかった, よろしい 名 ①善, 徳, 益, 幸福 ②《-s》財産, 品, 物質 **Good heavens!** まさか！, しまった！

□ **good-bye** 間さようなら 名別れのあいさつ

□ **goodbye** 間さようなら 名別れのあいさつ

□ **got** 動get（得る）の過去, 過去分詞

□ **grandfather** 名祖父

□ **grateful** 形感謝する, ありがたく思う

□ **ground** 名地面, 土, 土地 **fall to the ground** 転ぶ **ground floor** 1階 動 ①基づかせる ②着陸する ③grind（ひく）の過去, 過去分詞 形（粉に）ひいた, すった

□ **guess** 動 ①推測する, 言い当て

る ②(～と)思う 名推定, 憶測

□ **gun** 名銃, 大砲 動銃で撃つ

□ **gypsy** 名①ジプシー, ロマ民族の人 ②〔自由に生きる〕放浪人 ③〔仕事で移り住むことが多い〕大学非常勤教員, コーラス[ダンサー]団員

H

□ **had** 動have(持つ)の過去, 過去分詞 助haveの過去《過去完了の文をつくる》

□ **hair** 名髪, 毛

□ **half** 名半分 形半分の, 不完全な 副半分, なかば, 不十分に **in half** 〔切り方などが〕半分に, 2等分に

□ **hall** 名公会堂, ホール, 大広間, 玄関

□ **hallway** 名玄関, 廊下

□ **hand** 名①手 ②(時計の)針 ③援助の手, 助け **shake hands** 握手する 動手渡す

□ **handkerchief** 名ハンカチ

□ **hang** 動かかる, かける, つるす, ぶら下がる 名①かかり具合 ②《the –》扱い方, こつ

□ **happen** 動①(出来事が)起こる, 生じる ②偶然[たまたま]～する **happen to** たまたま～する, 偶然～する

□ **happy** 形幸せな, うれしい, 幸運な, 満足して **happy to do**《be –》～してうれしい, 喜んで～する

□ **hard** 形①堅い ②激しい, むずかしい ③熱心な, 勤勉な ④無情な, 耐えがたい, 厳しい, きつい 副①一生懸命に ②激しく ③堅く

□ **Harrow** 名ハロー《ロンドンの地名》

□ **has** 動have(持つ)の3人称単数現在 助haveの3人称単数現在《現在完了の文をつくる》

□ **have** 動①持つ, 持っている, 抱く ②(～が)ある, いる ③食べる, 飲む ④経験する, (病気に)かかる ⑤催す, 開く ⑥(人に) ～させる **have to** ～しなければならない 助《〈have＋過去分詞〉の形で現在完了の文をつくる》～した, ～したことがある, ずっと～している **have a headache** 頭痛がする **have been to** ～へ行ったことがある **would have … if ～** もし～だったとしたら…しただろう

□ **he** 代彼は[が]

□ **head** 名①頭 ②先頭 ③長, 指導者 **head of** ～の長 動向かう, 向ける

□ **headache** 名頭痛 **have a headache** 頭痛がする

□ **healthy** 形健康な, 健全な, 健康によい

□ **hear** 動聞く, 聞こえる **hear of** ～について聞く

□ **heard** 動hear(聞く)の過去, 過去分詞

□ **heaven** 名①天国 ②天国のようなところ[状態], 楽園 ③空 ④《H-》神 **Good heavens!** まさか!, しまった!

□ **heavy** 形重い, 激しい, つらい

□ **held** 動hold(つかむ)の過去, 過去分詞

□ **Helen Stoner** ヘレン・ストーナー《人名》

□ **help** 動 ①助ける, 手伝う ②給仕する 名 助け, 手伝い

□ **helper** 名 助手, 助けになるもの

□ **her** 代 ①彼女を[に] ②彼女の

□ **here** 副 ①ここに[で] ②《- is [are] ～》ここに～がある ③さあ, そら **here is ～** こちらは～です。 名 ここ

□ **him** 代 彼を[に]

□ **himself** 代 彼自身

□ **his** 代 ①彼の ②彼のもの

□ **hiss** 動 (シューと)音を出す, シーッと言う 名 シューという音

□ **hit** 動 ①打つ, なぐる ②ぶつける, ぶつかる ③命中する ④(天災などが)襲う, 打撃を与える ⑤hitの過去, 過去分詞 名 ①打撃 ②命中 ③大成功

□ **hold someone in one's arms** (人)を抱き締める

□ **hole** 名 ①穴, すき間 ②苦境, 困難 動 穴をあける, 穴に入る[入れる]

□ **home** 名 ①家, 自国, 故郷, 家庭 ②収容所 副 家に, 自国へ **at home** 自宅で, 在宅して, くつろいで **go home** 帰宅する 形 家の, 家庭の, 地元の 動 ①家[本国]に帰る ②(飛行機などを)誘導する

□ **hope** 名 希望, 期待, 見込み 動 望む, (～であるようにと)思う

□ **hospital** 名 病院

□ **hour** 名 1時間, 時間

□ **house** 名 ①家, 家庭 ②(特定の目的のための)建物, 小屋

□ **how** 副 ①どうやって, どれくらい, どんなふうに ②なんて(～だろう) ③《関係副詞》～する方法 **How about ～?** ～はどうですか。～しませんか。 **How could ～?** 何だって～なんてことがありえようか? **how to** ～する方法 **tell ～ how to** … ～に…のやり方を教える

□ **however** 副 たとえ～でも 接 けれども, だが

□ **huge** 形 巨大な, ばく大な

□ **hundred** 名 ①100(の数字), 100人[個] ②《-s》何百, 多数 形 ①100の, 100人[個]の ②多数の **hundreds of** 何百もの～

□ **hunted** 形 追われた, やつれた

□ **hurt** 動 傷つける, 痛む, 害する 名 傷, けが, 苦痛, 害

I

□ **I** 代 私は[が] **I wish ～** ～だったらよかったのに。

□ **idea** 名 考え, 意見, アイデア, 計画

□ **if** 接 もし～ならば, たとえ～でも, ～かどうか **would have … if ～** もし～だったとしたら…しただろう 名 疑問, 条件, 仮定

□ **imagine** 動 想像する, 心に思い描く

□ **immediately** 副 すぐに, ～するやいなや

□ **important** 形 重要な, 大切な, 有力な

□ **impressed** 形 印象付けられて,

A B C D E F G H I J K L M N O P Q R S T U V W X Y Z

感動して，感銘を受けて

- □ **in** 前 ①《場所・位置・所属》～(の中)に[で・の] ②《時》～(の時)に[の・で]，～後(に)，～の間(に) ③《方法・手段》～で ④～を身につけて，～を着て ⑤～に関して，～について ⑥《状態》～の状態で 副 中へ[に]，内へ[に]
- □ **income** 名 収入，所得，収益
- □ **India** 名 インド《国名》
- □ **information** 名 ①情報，通知，知識 ②案内(所)，受付(係)
- □ **ink** 名 インク 動 (ペンなどに)インクをつける
- □ **inn** 名 宿屋，居酒屋
- □ **inside** 名 内部，内側 形 内部[内側]にある 副 内部[内側]に 前 ～の内部[内側]に
- □ **instead** 副 その代わりに **instead of** ～の代わりに
- □ **interested** 動 interest(興味を起こさせる)の過去，過去分詞 形 興味を持った，関心のある **interested in**《be –》～に興味[関心]がある
- □ **interesting** 動 interest(興味を起こさせる)の現在分詞 形 おもしろい，興味を起こさせる
- □ **interrupt** 動 さえぎる，妨害する，口をはさむ
- □ **interview** 名 会見，面接 動 会見[面接]する
- □ **into** 前 ①《動作・運動の方向》～の中へ[に] ②《変化》～に[へ]
- □ **introduce** 動 紹介する，採り入れる，導入する
- □ **irish-setter** 名 アイリッシュ・セッター《犬種の一つ。レッド・セッターとも呼ばれ、毛が赤い色をしている》
- □ **iron** 名 ①鉄，鉄製のもの ②アイロン 形 鉄の，鉄製の 動 アイロンをかける
- □ **is** 動 be(～である)の3人称単数現在
- □ **it** 代 ①それは[が]，それを[に] ②《天候・日時・距離・寒暖などを示す》
- □ **its** 代 それの，あれの
- □ **itself** 代 それ自体，それ自身

J

- □ **Jabez Wilson** ジェイベズ・ウィルソン《人名》
- □ **job** 名 仕事，職，雇用
- □ **John Clay** ジョン・クレイ《人名》
- □ **join** 動 ①一緒になる，参加する ②連結[結合]する，つなぐ 名 結合
- □ **Jones** 名 ジョーンズ《人名》
- □ **joy** 名 喜び，楽しみ
- □ **jump** 動 ①跳ぶ，跳躍する，飛び越える，飛びかかる ②(～を)熱心にやり始める **jump up** 素早く立ち上がる 名 ①跳躍 ②急騰，急転
- □ **just** 形 正しい，もっともな，当然な 副 ①まさに，ちょうど，(～した)ばかり ②ほんの，単に，ただ～だけ ③ちょっと **Just a minute.** ちょっと待って。 **just then** そのとたんに

K

- □ **keep** 動 ①とっておく，保つ，続ける ②(～を…に)しておく ③飼

う，養う ④経営する ⑤守る

□ **kept** 動 keep（とっておく）の過去，過去分詞

□ **kettle** 名 なべ，やかん

□ **kind** 形 親切な，優しい 名 種類 **kind of** ある程度，いくらか，～のようなもの［人］

□ **kindly** 形 ①親切な，情け深い，思いやりのある ②（気候などの）温和な，快い 副 親切に，優しく

□ **king** 名 王，国王

□ **King Edward Street** キング・エドワード・ストリート《ロンドンにある通り》

□ **knee** 名 ひざ

□ **knew** 動 know（知っている）の過去

□ **knife** 名 ナイフ，小刀，包丁，短剣

□ **knock** 動 ノックする，たたく，ぶつける 名 打つこと，戸をたたくこと［音］

□ **know** 動 ①知っている，知る，（～が）わかる，理解している ②知り合いである

□ **knowing** 動 know（知っている）の現在分詞 形 物知りの，故意の

□ **known** 動 know（知っている）の過去分詞 形 知られた

L

□ **laborer** 名 労働者

□ **lady** 名 婦人，夫人，淑女，奥さん

□ **lamp** 名 ランプ，灯火

□ **land** 名 ①陸地，土地 ②国，領域 動 上陸する，着地する

□ **large** 形 ①大きい，広い ②大勢の，多量の 副 ①大きく ②自慢して

□ **last** 形 ①《the –》最後の ②この前の，先～ ③最新の 副 ①最後に ②この前 **at last** ついに，とうとう 名《the –》最後（のもの），終わり 動 続く，持ちこたえる

□ **late** 形 ①遅い，後期の ②最近の ③《the –》故～ 副 ①遅れて，遅く ②最近まで，以前

□ **later** 形 もっと遅い，もっと後の 副 後で，後ほど

□ **laugh** 動 笑う **break out laughing** どっと笑い出す 名 笑い（声）

□ **lawyer** 名 弁護士，法律家

□ **lead someone down** （人）を～に案内する［連れて行く］

□ **league** 名 ①同盟，連盟 ②（スポーツの）競技連盟

□ **learn** 動 学ぶ，習う，教わる，知識［経験］を得る

□ **leash** 名 （動物をつなぐ）皮ひも，鎖

□ **least** 形 いちばん小さい，最も少ない 副 いちばん小さく，最も少なく **at least** 少なくとも 名 最小，最少

□ **leave** 動 ①出発する，去る ②残す，置き忘れる ③（～を…の）ままにしておく ④ゆだねる **leave the rest to** 残りは（人）に任せる 名 ①休暇 ②許可 ③別れ

□ **leaves** 名 leaf（葉）の複数 動 leave（出発する）の３人称単数現在

□ **led** 動 lead（導く）の過去，過去分

詞

□ **left** 名《the –》左, 左側 形左の, 左側の 副左に, 左側に 動leave(去る, ～をあとに残す)の過去, 過去分詞

□ **less** 形 ～より小さい[少ない] 副 ～より少なく, ～ほどでなく

□ **let** 動(人に～)させる, (～するのを)許す, (～をある状態に)する **let us** どうか私たちに～させてください

□ **letter** 名 ①手紙 ②文字 ③文学, 文筆業

□ **life** 名 ①生命, 生物 ②一生, 生涯, 人生 ③生活, 暮らし, 世の中

□ **light** 名光, 明かり 動火をつける, 照らす, 明るくする 形 ①明るい ②(色が)薄い, 淡い ③軽い, 容易な 副軽く, 容易に

□ **like** 動好む, 好きである 前 ～に似ている, ～のような 形似ている, ～のような 接あたかも～のように **like this** このような, こんなふうに **look like** ～のように見える, ～に似ている **would like to** ～したいと思う

□ **line** 名 ①線, 糸, 電話線 ②(字の)行 ③列, (電車の) ～線 動 ①線を引く ②整列する

□ **listen** 動《– to ～》～を聞く, ～に耳を傾ける

□ **lit** 動light(火をつける)の過去, 過去分詞

□ **little** 形 ①小さい, 幼い ②少しの, 短い ③ほとんど～ない, 《a –》少しはある 名少し(しか), 少量 副全然～ない, 《a –》少しはある

□ **live** 動住む, 暮らす, 生きている 形 ①生きている, 生きた ②ライブの, 実況の 副生で, ライブで

□ **liver** 名肝臓

□ **lives** 名life(生命)の複数

□ **local** 形 ①地方の, ある場所[土地]の, 部分的な ②各駅停車の 名ある特定の地方のもの

□ **lock** 名錠(前) 動錠を下ろす, 閉じ込める, 動けなくする

□ **London** 名ロンドン《英国の首都》

□ **lonely** 形 ①孤独な, 心さびしい ②ひっそりした, 人里離れた

□ **long** 形 ①長い, 長期の ②《長さ・距離・時間などを示す語句を伴って》～の長さ[距離・時間]の **any longer** これ以上, もっと長く 副長い間, ずっと 名長い期間 動切望する, 思い焦がれる

□ **look** 動 ①見る ②(～に)見える, (～の)顔つきをする ③注意する ④《間投詞のように》ほら, ねえ **look for** ～を探す **look into** ①～を調査する, 検討する ②～の中を見る, のぞき込む **look like** ～のように見える, ～に似ている **look up** 見上げる, 調べる 名 ①一見, 目つき ②外観, 外見, 様子

□ **lose** 動 ①失う, 迷う, 忘れる ②負ける, 失敗する

□ **lost** 動lose(失う)の過去, 過去分詞 形 ①失った, 負けた ②道に迷った, 困った ③没頭している

□ **lot** 名 ①くじ, 運 ②地所, 区画 ③たくさん, たいへん, 《a – of ～/ -s of ～》たくさんの～ ④やつ, 連中

□ **loudly** 副大声で，騒がしく

□ **love** 名愛，愛情，思いやり 動愛する，恋する，大好きである

□ **lucky** 形幸運な，運のよい，縁起のよい

□ **lunch** 名昼食，ランチ，軽食

M

□ **madam** 名《ていねいな呼びかけ》奥様，お嬢様

□ **made** 動make（作る）の過去，過去分詞 形作った，作られた

□ **magic** 名 ①魔法，手品 ②魔力 形魔法の，魔力のある

□ **make** 動 ①作る，得る ②行う，（～に）なる ③（～を…に）する，（～を…）させる

□ **making** 動make（作る）の現在分詞 名制作，製造

□ **man** 名男性，人，人類 **fine man** 立派な男性

□ **many** 形多数の，たくさんの 代多数（の人・物） **so many** 非常に多くの

□ **march** 名 ①行進 ②《M-》3月 動行進する［させる］，進展する

□ **mark** 名 ①印，記号，跡 ②点数 ③特色 動 ①印［記号］をつける ②採点する ③目立たせる

□ **marriage** 名 ①結婚（生活・式） ②結合，融合，（吸収）合併

□ **married** 動marry（結婚する）の過去，過去分詞 形結婚した，既婚の

□ **marry** 動結婚する

□ **match** 名 ①試合，勝負 ②相手，釣り合うもの ③マッチ（棒） 動 ①～に匹敵する ②調和する，釣り合う ③（～を…と）勝負させる

□ **matchbox** 名マッチ箱

□ **may** 助 ①～かもしれない ②～してもよい，～できる 名《M-》5月

□ **maybe** 副たぶん，おそらく

□ **me** 代私を［に］ **Dear me!** おや！，まあ！《驚きを表す》

□ **mean** 動 ①意味する ②（～のつもりで）言う，意図する ③～するつもりである **mean A by B** Aという意味でBと言う 形 ①卑怯な，けちな，意地悪な ②中間の 名中間，中位

□ **meant** 動mean（意味する）の過去，過去分詞

□ **meet** 動 ①会う，知り合いになる ②合流する，交わる ③（条件などに）達する，合う

□ **men** 名man（男性）の複数

□ **mention** 動（～について）述べる，言及する 名言及，陳述

□ **Merryweather** 名メリーウェザー《人名》

□ **met** 動meet（会う）の過去，過去分詞

□ **metal** 名金属，合金

□ **metallic** 形金属の，金属性の

□ **midday** 名正午，真昼

□ **milk** 名牛乳，ミルク 動乳をしぼる

□ **millionaire** 名百万長者，大金持ち

□ **mind** 名 ①心，精神，考え ②知

性 動 ①気にする，いやがる ②気をつける，用心する

□ **mine** 代 私のもの 名 鉱山 動 採掘する，坑道を掘る

□ **minute** 名 ①（時間の）分 ②ちょっとの間 **Just a minute.** ちょっと待って。 形 ごく小さい，細心の

□ **miss** 動 ①失敗する，免れる，～を見逃す，（目標を）はずす ②（～が）ないのに気づく，（人が）いなくてさびしく思う 名 ①はずれ，失敗 ②《M-》《女性に対して》～さん，～先生

□ **moment** 名 ①瞬間，ちょっとの間 ②（特定の）時，時期 **one moment** ちょっとの間

□ **Monday** 名 月曜日

□ **money** 名 金，通貨

□ **month** 名 月，1カ月

□ **more** 形 ①もっと多くの ②それ以上の，余分の 副 もっと，さらに多く，いっそう **more than** ～以上 名 もっと多くの物[人]

□ **morning** 名 朝，午前

□ **mortgage** 名 抵当（権） 動 抵当に入れる

□ **most** 形 ①最も多い ②たいていの，大部分の 代 ①大部分，ほとんど ②最多数，最大限 副 最も（多く）

□ **mostly** 副 主として，多くは，ほとんど

□ **mother** 名 母，母親

□ **move** 動 ①動く，動かす ②感動させる ③引っ越す，移動する **move along** ～に沿って動く **move into** 入居する 名 ①動き，運動 ②転居，移動

□ **Mr.** 名《男性に対して》～さん，～氏，～先生

□ **much** 形（量・程度が）多くの，多量の 副 ①とても，たいへん ②《比較級・最上級を修飾して》ずっと，はるかに 名 多量，たくさん，重要なもの

□ **muscle** 名 筋肉，腕力 動 強引に押し進む，力ずくで進む

□ **music** 名 音楽，楽曲

□ **must** 助 ①～しなければならない ②～に違いない 名 絶対に必要なこと[もの]

□ **my** 代 私の

□ **myself** 代 私自身

□ **mystery** 名 ①神秘，不可思議 ②推理小説，ミステリー

N

□ **name** 名 ①名前 ②名声 ③《-s》悪口 動 ①名前をつける ②名指しする

□ **near** 前 ～の近くに，～のそばに 形 近い，親しい 副 近くに，親密で

□ **need** 動（～を）必要とする，必要である 助 ～する必要がある **need to do** ～する必要がある 名 ①必要（性），《-s》必要なもの ②まさかの時

□ **neighborhood** 名 近所（の人々），付近

□ **nervous** 形 ①神経の ②神経質な，おどおどした

□ **never** 副 決して[少しも] ～ない，一度も[二度と] ～ない

□ **new** 形 ①新しい，新規の ②新鮮

な，できたての

□ **newspaper** 名 新聞（紙）

□ **next** 形 ①次の，翌～ ②隣の 副 ①次に ②隣に **next to** ～のとなりに，～の次に 代 次の人［もの］

□ **nice** 形 すてきな，よい，きれいな，親切な

□ **night** 名 夜，晩

□ **nightfall** 名 夕暮れ

□ **nine** 名 9（の数字），9人［個］ 形 9の，9人［個］の

□ **no** 副 ①いいえ，いや ②少しも～ない 形 ～がない，少しも～ない，～どころでない，～禁止 **no one** 誰も［一人も］～ない 名 否定，拒否

□ **noise** 名 騒音，騒ぎ，物音

□ **noon** 名 ①正午，真昼 ②《the －》全盛期

□ **normal** 形 普通の，平均の，標準的な 名 平常，標準，典型

□ **not** 副 ～でない，～しない **better not** ～しない方がよい **Not at all.** 全くそんなことはありません。どういたしまして。 **not ～ at all** 全く～でない **not ～ but …** ～ではなくて…

□ **note** 名 ①メモ，覚え書き ②注釈 ③注意，注目 ④手形 動 ①書き留める ②注意［注目］する

□ **nothing** 代 何も～ない［しない］

□ **notice** 名 ①注意 ②通知 ③公告 動 ①気づく，認める ②通告する

□ **now** 副 ①今（では），現在 ②今すぐに ③では，さて 名 今，現在 形 今の，現在の **for now** 今のところ，ひとまず **now that** 今や～だから，～からには **That is all for now.** 今のところ以上です。

□ **number** 名 ①数，数字，番号 ②～号，～番 ③《-s》多数 動 番号をつける，数える

O

□ **o'clock** 副 ～時

□ **October** 名 10月

□ **of** 前 ①《所有・所属・部分》～の，～に属する ②《性質・特徴・材料》～の，～製の ③《部分》～のうち ④《分離・除去》～から

□ **off** 副 ①離れて ②はずれて ③止まって ④休んで 形 ①離れて ②季節はずれの ③休みの 前 ～を離れて，～をはずれて，（値段が）～引きの **day off work**《a －》〔平日に取る〕休日 **take off**（衣服を）脱ぐ，～を取り除く

□ **office** 名 ①会社，事務所，職場，役所，局 ②官職，地位，役

□ **officer** 名 役人，公務員，警察官

□ **often** 副 しばしば，たびたび

□ **oh** 間 ああ，おや，まあ

□ **old** 形 ①年取った，老いた ②～歳の ③古い，昔の 名 昔，老人

□ **on** 前 ①《場所・接触》～（の上）に ②《日・時》～に，～と同時に，～のすぐ後で ③《関係・従事》～に関して，～について，～して 副 ①身につけて，上に ②前へ，続けて **on the way** 途中で

□ **once** 副 ①一度，1回 ②かつて 名 一度，1回 接 いったん～すると

□ **one** 名 1（の数字），1人［個］

形 ①1の, 1人[個]の ②ある～ ③《the –》唯一の 代 ①(一般の)人, ある物 ②一方, 片方 ③～なもの **no one** 誰も[一人も]～ない **one day** (過去の)ある日, (未来の)いつか **one moment** ちょっとの間 **one of** ～の1つ[人] **one side** 片側

□ **oneself** 熟 **for oneself** 独力で, 自分のために **throw oneself down on** ～に身を投げ出す, 寝転がる

□ **only** 形 唯一の 副 ①単に, ～にすぎない, ただ～だけ ②やっと 接 ただし, だがしかし

□ **open** 形 ①開いた, 広々とした ②公開された 動 ①開く, 始まる ②広がる, 広げる ③打ち明ける **open fire** 発砲を開始する **open into** ～に開口している

□ **opening** 動 open (開く)の現在分詞 名 ①開始, 始め ②開いた所, 穴 ③空き, 欠員 形 開始の, 最初の, 開会の

□ **opinion** 名 意見, 見識, 世論, 評判

□ **or** 接 ①～か…, または ②さもないと ③すなわち, 言い換えると

□ **orange** 名 オレンジ 形 オレンジ色の

□ **organization** 名 ①組織(化), 編成, 団体, 機関 ②有機体, 生物

□ **other** 形 ①ほかの, 異なった ②(2つのうち)もう一方の, (3つ以上のうち)残りの 代 ①ほかの人[物] ②《the –》残りの1つ **enjoy each other's company** お互いに楽しくやる

□ **our** 代 私たちの

□ **out** 副 ①外へ[に], 不在で, 離れて ②世に出て ③消えて ④すっかり 形 ①外の, 遠く離れた ②公表された 前 ～から外へ[に] 動 ①追い出す ②露見する **break out laughing** どっと笑い出す **come out of** ①～から出てくる ②～から採れる, 産出される **cry out** 叫ぶ **figure out** 理解する, (原因などを)解明する, 見当がつく **get out of** ～から下車する **get ～ out of the way** ～を追い出す, どかす **out of** ①～から外へ, ～から抜け出して ②～の範囲外に, ～から離れて **run out of** ～から駆け出す, ～から逃げ出す

□ **outside** 名 外部, 外側 形 外部の, 外側の 副 外へ, 外側に 前 ～の外に[で・の・へ], ～の範囲を越えて

□ **over** 前 ①～の上の[に], ～を一面に覆って ②～を越えて, ～以上に, ～よりまさって ③～の向こう側の[に] ④～の間 副 上に, 一面に, ずっと 形 ①上部の, 上位の, 過多の ②終わって, すんで **all over** すっかり[全て]終わって **go over to** ～の前に[へ]行く, ～に出向いて行く **walk over** ～の方に歩いていく

□ **own** 形 自身の 動 持っている, 所有する

□ **owner** 名 持ち主, オーナー

□ **Oxford** 名《– University》オックスフォード大学

P

□ **page** 名 ページ

□ **paid** 動 pay (払う)の過去, 過去

分詞 形有給の, 支払い済みのの

□ **pain** 名 ①痛み, 苦悩 ②《-s》骨折り, 苦労 動苦痛を与える, 痛む

□ **paint** 動 ①ペンキを塗る ②(絵の具などで)描く 名塗料, ペンキ, 絵の具

□ **pale** 形 ①(顔色・人が)青ざめた, 青白い ②(色が)薄い, (光が)薄暗い 動 ①青ざめる, 青ざめさせる ②淡くなる[する], 色あせる

□ **paper** 名 ①紙 ②新聞, 論文, 答案 ③《-s》書類 ④紙幣, 手形 **writing paper** 便せん, 筆記[メモ]用紙

□ **pass** 動 ①過ぎる, 通る ②(年月が)たつ ③(試験に)合格する ④手渡す **pass through** ～を通る, 貫通する

□ **pause** 名 ①(活動の)中止, 休止 ②区切り 動休止する, 立ち止まる

□ **pawnshop** 名質屋

□ **pay** 動 ①支払う, 払う, 報いる, 償う ②割に合う, ペイする 名給料, 報い

□ **payday** 名給料日

□ **payment** 名支払い, 払い込み

□ **pen** 名①ペン ②文筆, 文体 ③囲い, おり 動囲い[おり]に入れる

□ **people** 名 ①(一般に)人々 ②民衆, 世界の人々, 国民, 民族 ③人間

□ **perfect** 形 ①完璧な, 完全な ②純然たる 動完成する, 改良[改善]する

□ **person** 名 ①人 ②人格, 人柄 **in person** (本人)自ら, 自身で

□ **personally** 副個人的には, 自分で

□ **pick** 動 ①(花・果実などを)摘む, もぐ ②選ぶ, 精選する ③つつく, つついて穴をあける, ほじくり出す ④(～を)摘み取る **pick up** 拾い上げる 名 ①《the –》精選したもの ②選択(権) ③つつくもの, つるはし

□ **picture** 名 ①絵, 写真, 《-s》映画 ②イメージ, 事態, 状況, 全体像 **take a picture** 写真を撮る 動描く, 想像する

□ **piece** 名 ①一片, 部分 ②1個, 1本 ③作品

□ **pierced** 形〔イヤリングなどを付けるための〕穴を開けた, ピアスをした

□ **pink** 形ピンク色の 名ピンク色

□ **place** 名 ①場所, 建物 ②余地, 空間 ③《one's -》家, 部屋 **take place** 行われる, 起こる 動 ①置く, 配置する ②任命する, 任じる

□ **plan** 名計画, 設計(図), 案 動計画する

□ **play** 動 ①遊ぶ, 競技する ②(楽器を)演奏する, (役を)演じる **play cards** トランプ[で賭け]をする 名遊び, 競技, 劇

□ **please** 動喜ばす, 満足させる 間どうぞ, お願いします

□ **pleased** 動please(喜ばす)の過去, 過去分詞 形喜んだ, 気に入った **pleased with** 《be –》～が気に入る

□ **pocket** 名 ①ポケット, 袋 ②所持金 動 ①ポケットに入れる ②着服する 形携帯用の, 小型の

□ **point** 名 ①先, 先端 ②点 ③地点, 時点, 箇所 ④《the –》要点 **at this point** 現在のところ, この時点では

動 ①(～を)指す, 向ける ②とがらせる

□ **pointed** 動 point(指す)の過去, 過去分詞 形 先のとがった, 鋭い

□ **poison** 名 ①毒, 毒薬 ②害になるもの 動 毒を盛る, 毒する

□ **poker** 名 ①(トランプで)ポーカー ②火かき棒

□ **police** 名 ①《the –》警察, 警官 ②公安, 治安 動 警備する, 治安を維持する

□ **policeman** 名 警察官

□ **possible** 形 ①可能な ②ありうる, 起こりうる **as soon as possible** できるだけ早く, 速やかに

□ **pound** 名 ①ポンド《英国の通貨単位》 ②ポンド《重量の単位。453.6g》 動 どんどんたたく, 打ち砕く

□ **power** 名 力, 能力, 才能, 勢力, 権力

□ **present** 形 ①出席している, ある, いる ②現在の 動 ①紹介する ②現れる ③与える ④提出する, 述べる, 示す

□ **prevent** 動 ①妨げる, じゃまする ②予防する, 守る, 《– ～ from …》～が…できない[しない]ようにする

□ **prison** 名 ①刑務所, 監獄 ②監禁

□ **privately** 副 内密に, 非公式に, 個人的に

□ **problem** 名 問題, 難問

□ **proof** 名 ①証拠, 証明 ②試し, 吟味

□ **protect** 動 保護する, 防ぐ

□ **pull** 動 ①引く, 引っ張る ②引きつける **pull on** ～を引っ張る, たぐり寄せる 名 ①引くこと ②縁故, こね

□ **push** 動 ①押す, 押し進む, 押し進める ②進む, 突き出る **push back** 押し返す, 押しのける **push through** (人ごみなどを)かき分ける 名 押し, 突進, 後援

□ **put** 動 ①置く, のせる ②入れる, つける ③(ある状態に)する ④put の過去, 過去分詞 **put in** ～の中に入れる, ～に取り付ける **put on** ～を…の上に置く **put ～ back** ～を(もとの場所に)戻す, 返す **put ～ into …** ～を…の状態にする, ～を…に突っ込む

Q

□ **qualified** 動 qualify(資格を得る)の過去, 過去分詞 形 資格のある, 免許を受けた

□ **question** 名 質問, 疑問, 問題 動 ①質問する ②調査する ③疑う

□ **quick** 形 (動作が)速い, すばやい 副 速く, 急いで, すぐに

□ **quickly** 副 敏速に, 急いで

□ **quiet** 形 ①静かな, 穏やかな, じっとした ②おとなしい, 無口な, 目立たない 名 静寂, 平穏 動 静まる, 静める

□ **quietly** 副 ①静かに ②平穏に, 控えめに

□ **quite** 副 ①まったく, すっかり, 完全に ②かなり, ずいぶん ③ほとんど

R

□ **rain** 名雨, 降雨 動①雨が降る ②雨のように降る[降らせる]

□ **ran** 動run (走る) の過去

□ **reach** 動①着く, 到着する, 届く ②手を伸ばして取る 名手を伸ばすこと, (手の) 届く範囲

□ **read** 動読む, 読書する

□ **ready** 形用意[準備]ができた, まさに～しようとする, 今にも～せんばかりの **ready for** 《be –》準備が整って, ～に期待する 動用意[準備]する

□ **real** 形実際の, 実在する, 本物の 副本当に

□ **realize** 動理解する, 実現する

□ **really** 副本当に, 実際に, 確かに

□ **reason** 名①理由 ②理性, 道理 動①推論する ②説き伏せる

□ **reasoning** 名①論法, 推理, 推論 ②論拠, 根拠

□ **recently** 副近ごろ, 最近

□ **red** 形赤い 名赤, 赤色 **turn red** 赤くなる

□ **red-headed** 形赤毛の, 赤い頭髪の

□ **religious** 形①宗教の ②信心深い

□ **repay** 動①払い戻す, 返金する ②報いる, 恩返しする

□ **reply** 動答える, 返事をする, 応答する 名答え, 返事, 応答

□ **responsible** 形責任のある, 信頼できる, 確実な **responsible for** 《be –》～に対して責任がある

□ **rest** 名①休息 ②安静 ③休止, 停止 ④《the –》残り **leave the rest to** 残りは(人)に任せる 動①休む, 眠る ②休止する, 静止する ③(～に)基づいている ④(～の)ままである

□ **return** 動帰る, 戻る, 返す 名①帰還, 返却 ②返答, 報告(書), 申告 形①帰りの, 往復の ②お返しの

□ **rich** 形①富んだ, 金持ちの ②豊かな, 濃い, 深い 名裕福な人

□ **right** 形①正しい ②適切な ③健全な ④右(側)の **all right** 大丈夫で, よろしい, わかった 副①まっすぐに, すぐに ②右(側)に ③ちょうど, 正確に 名①正しいこと ②権利 ③《the –》右, ライト

□ **rob** 動奪う, 金品を盗む, 襲う

□ **robbery** 名泥棒, 強盗

□ **room** 名①部屋 ②空間, 余地 **strong room** 金庫室

□ **rope** 名綱, なわ, ロープ 動なわで縛る

□ **run** 動①走る ②運行する ③(川が)流れる ④経営する **run down** 駆け下りる **run out of** ～から駆け出す, ～から逃げ出す 名①走ること, 競走 ②連続, 続き ③得点

□ **running** 動run (走る) の現在分詞 名ランニング, 競走 形①走っている ②上演中の ③連続する **come running from** ～から飛んでくる, かけつける

S

□ **sad** 形①悲しい, 悲しげな ②惨

めな, 不運な

□ **safe** 形 ①安全な, 危険のない ②用心深い, 慎重な 名 金庫

□ **said** 動 say（言う）の過去, 過去分詞

□ **same** 形 ①同じ, 同様の ②前述の **in the same way** 同様に 代《the –》同一の人［物］ 副《the –》同様に

□ **sat** 動 sit（座る）の過去, 過去分詞

□ **satisfied** 動 satisfy（満足させる）の過去, 過去分詞 形 満足した **satisfied with**《be –》～に満足する

□ **Saturday** 名 土曜日

□ **save** 動 ①救う, 守る ②とっておく, 節約する

□ **saw** 動 ①see（見る）の過去 ②のこぎりで切る, のこぎりを使う 名 のこぎり

□ **say** 動 言う, 口に出す 名 言うこと, 言い分 間 さあ, まあ

□ **saying** 動 say（言う）の現在分詞 名 ことわざ, 格言, 発言

□ **Scotland Yard** スコットランドヤード, ロンドン警視庁

□ **scream** 名 金切り声, 絶叫 動 叫ぶ, 金切り声を出す

□ **second** 名 ①第2（の人［物］） ②（時間の）秒, 瞬時 形 第2の, 2番の 副 第2に

□ **secret** 形 ①秘密の, 隠れた ②神秘の, 不思議な 名 秘密, 神秘

□ **see** 動 ①見る, 見える, 見物する ②（～と）わかる, 認識する, 経験する ③会う ④考える, 確かめる, 調べる ⑤気をつける **see that**（～するように）気を付ける **you see** あのね, いいですか

□ **seem** 動（～に）見える,（～のように）思われる **seem to be** ～であるように思われる

□ **seen** 動 see（見る）の過去分詞

□ **send ~ away** ～を追い払う, 送り出す

□ **sent** 動 send（送る）の過去, 過去分詞

□ **serious** 形 ①まじめな, 真剣な ②重大な, 深刻な,（病気などが）重い

□ **servant** 名 ①召使, 使用人, しもべ ②公務員,（公共事業の）従業員

□ **seven** 名 7（の数字）, 7人［個］ 形 7の, 7人［個］の

□ **shake** 動 ①振る, 揺れる, 揺さぶる, 震える ②動揺させる **shake hands** 握手する 名 振ること

□ **shall** 助 ①《Iが主語で》～するだろう, ～だろう ②《I以外が主語で》（…に）～させよう,（…は）～することになるだろう

□ **she** 代 彼女は［が］

□ **sheet** 名 ①シーツ ②（紙などの）1枚

□ **Sherlock Holmes** シャーロック・ホームズ《人名》

□ **shiny** 形 輝く, 光る

□ **shiver** 動（寒さなどで）身震いする, 震える 名 震え, 悪寒

□ **shock** 名 衝撃, ショック **in shock**《be –》ショックを受けている 動 ショックを与える

□ **shocked** 形 ～にショックを受け

A B C D E F G H I J K L M N O P Q R S T U V W X Y Z

て，憤慨して

- ☐ **shook** 動 shake（振る）の過去
- ☐ **shoot** 動 ①（銃を）撃つ ②放つ，噴出する
- ☐ **shop** 名 ①店，小売り店 ②仕事場 動 買い物をする
- ☐ **short** 形 ①短い ②背の低い ③不足している 副 ①手短に，簡単に ②不足して
- ☐ **should** 助 ～すべきである，～したほうがよい
- ☐ **shout** 動 叫ぶ，大声で言う，どなりつける 名 叫び，大声，悲鳴
- ☐ **show** 動 ①見せる，示す，見える ②明らかにする，教える ③案内する 名 ①表示，見世物，ショー ②外見，様子
- ☐ **shut** 動 ①閉まる，閉める，閉じる ②たたむ ③閉じ込める ④shutの過去，過去分詞
- ☐ **side** 名 側，横，そば，斜面 **one side** 片側 形 ①側面の，横の ②副次的な 動（～の）側につく，賛成する
- ☐ **sign** 名 ①きざし，徴候 ②跡 ③記号 ④身振り，合図，看板 動 ①署名する，サインする ②合図する
- ☐ **similar** 形 同じような，類似した，相似の
- ☐ **simple** 形 ①単純な，簡単な，質素な ②単一の，単独の ③普通の，ただの
- ☐ **simply** 副 ①簡単に ②単に，ただ ③まったく，完全に
- ☐ **single** 形 ①たった1つの ②1人用の，それぞれの ③独身の ④片道の
- ☐ **sir** 名 ①あなた，先生《目上の男性，客などに対する呼びかけ》 ②拝啓《手紙の書き出し》
- ☐ **sister** 名 ①姉妹，姉，妹 ②修道女
- ☐ **sit** 動 ①座る，腰掛ける ②止まる ③位置する
- ☐ **six** 名 6（の数字），6人［個］ 形 6の，6人［個］の
- ☐ **sky** 名 ①空，天空，大空 ②天気，空模様，気候
- ☐ **sleep** 動 ①眠る，寝る ②活動しない 名 ①睡眠，冬眠 ②静止，不活動
- ☐ **sleeping** 形 眠っている，休止している 名 睡眠（状態），不活動
- ☐ **sleeve** 名 袖，たもと，スリーブ
- ☐ **slept** 動 sleep（眠る）の過去，過去分詞
- ☐ **slowly** 副 遅く，ゆっくり
- ☐ **small** 形 ①小さい，少ない ②取るに足りない 副 小さく，細かく
- ☐ **smart** 形 ①利口な，抜け目のない ②きちんとした，洗練された ③激しい，ずきずきする 動 ひりひり［ずきずき］痛む
- ☐ **smell** 動 ①（～の）においがする ②においをかぐ ③かぎつける，感づく 名 ①嗅覚 ②におい，香り
- ☐ **smile** 動 微笑する，にっこり笑う 名 微笑，ほほえみ
- ☐ **smoke** 動 喫煙する，煙を出す 名 煙，煙状のもの
- ☐ **snake** 名 ヘビ（蛇） 動（体を）くねらす，蛇行する

□ **sneak** 動 ①こそこそする ②こっそり持ち出す，くすねる **sneak into** ～に潜入する，～に忍び込む

□ **sneer** 動 冷笑する，あざ笑う，あざけって言う 名 冷笑

□ **snuck** 動 sneak（こそこそする）の過去・過去分詞形

□ **so** 副 ①とても ②同様に，～もまた ③《先行する句・節の代用》そのように，そう 接 ①だから，それで ②では，さて **so many** 非常に多くの **so that** ～するために，それで，～できるように **so ～ that …** 非常に～なので…

□ **soft** 形 ①柔らかい，手ざわり［口あたり］のよい ②温和な，落ち着いた ③（処分などが）厳しくない，手ぬるい，甘い

□ **solve** 動 解く，解決する

□ **some** 形 ①いくつかの，多少の ②ある，誰か，何か 副 約，およそ 代 ①いくつか ②ある人［物］たち

□ **someone** 代 ある人，誰か **get someone to do**（人）に～させる［してもらう］ **hold someone in one's arms**（人）を抱き締める **lead someone down**（人）を～に案内する［連れて行く］ **take someone away**（人）を連れ出す **talk to someone about** ～のことで（人）に話しかける

□ **something** 代 ①ある物，何か ②いくぶん，多少

□ **sometimes** 副 時々，時たま

□ **somewhere** 副 ①どこかへ［に］ ②いつか，およそ

□ **son** 名 息子，子弟，～の子

□ **soon** 副 まもなく，すぐに，すみやかに **as soon as possible** できるだけ早く，速やかに

□ **sorry** 形 気の毒に［申し訳なく］思う，残念な

□ **sound** 名 音，騒音，響き，サウンド 動 ①音がする，鳴る ②（～のように）思われる，（～と）聞こえる

□ **speckle** 名 斑点，ぽつぽつ，しみ 動 しみ［汚点，傷］をつける

□ **speckled** 形 たくさんの小さな斑点のついた

□ **spend** 動 ①（金などを）使う，消費［浪費］する ②（時を）過ごす

□ **spent** 動 spend（使う）の過去，過去分詞 形 使い果たした，疲れ切った

□ **spot** 名 ①地点，場所，立場 ②斑点，しみ 動 ①～を見つける ②点を打つ，しみをつける

□ **spring** 名 ①春 ②泉，源 ③ばね，ぜんまい 動 跳ねる，跳ぶ

□ **spy** 名 スパイ 動 ひそかに見張る，スパイする

□ **stand** 動 ①立つ，立たせる，立っている，ある ②耐える，立ち向かう **stand up** 立ち上がる

□ **stare** 動 じっと［じろじろ］見る 名 じっと見ること，凝視

□ **start** 動 ①出発する，始まる，始める ②生じる，生じさせる **start doing** ～し始める 名 出発，開始

□ **station** 名 ①駅 ②署，局，本部，部署 動 部署につかせる，配置する

□ **stay** 動 ①とどまる，泊まる，滞在する ②持続する，（～の）ままでいる **stay in** 家にいる，（場所）に泊ま

る，滞在する 名滞在

□ **steam** 名蒸気，湯気 動湯気を立てる

□ **stepfather** 名義父，継父

□ **stick** 名棒，杖 動①（突き）刺さる，刺す ②くっつく，くっつける ③突き出る ④《受け身形で》いきづまる

□ **still** 副①まだ，今でも ②それでも（なお） 形静止した，静かな

□ **stone** 名①石，小石 ②宝石 形石の，石製の

□ **stood** 動stand（立つ）の過去，過去分詞

□ **stop** 動①やめる，やめさせる，止める，止まる ②立ち止まる 名①停止 ②停留所，駅

□ **store** 名①店 ②蓄え ③貯蔵庫，倉庫 動蓄える，貯蔵する

□ **storm** 名①嵐，暴風雨 ②強襲 動①襲撃［強襲］する ②嵐が吹く ③突入する

□ **story** 名①物語，話 ②（建物の）階

□ **Strand** 名ストランド《ロンドンにある繁華街》

□ **strange** 形①知らない，見［聞き］慣れない ②奇妙な，変わった

□ **strawberry** 名イチゴ（苺）

□ **street** 名①街路 ②《S-》～通り

□ **strong** 形①強い，堅固な，強烈な ②濃い ③得意な 副強く，猛烈に **strong room** 金庫室

□ **study** 動①勉強する，研究する ②調べる 名①勉強，研究 ②書斎

□ **subway** 名地下鉄，地下道

□ **such** 形①そのような，このような ②そんなに，とても，非常に 代そのような人［物］ **such a** そのような

□ **suddenly** 副突然，急に

□ **sunny** 形①日当たりのよい，日のさす ②陽気な，快活な

□ **sure** 形確かな，確実な，《be – to ～》必ず［きっと］～する，確信して **sure about**《be – 》～に確信を持っている 副確かに，まったく，本当に

□ **surprised** 動surprise（驚かす）の過去，過去分詞 形驚いた **surprised to do**《be – 》～して驚く

□ **surrounding** 動surround（囲む）の現在分詞 名《-s》周囲の状況，環境 形周囲の

□ **swamp** 名沼地，（低）湿地 動①水浸しにする ②（仕事，物などが）押し寄せる，圧倒される

□ **swamp adder** 沼の毒ヘビ

□ **sweet** 形①甘い ②快い ③親切な ④かわいい，魅力的な

□ **sympathy** 名①同情，思いやり，お悔やみ ②共鳴，同感

T

□ **table** 名①テーブル，食卓，台 ②一覧表 動卓上に置く，棚上げにする

□ **take** 動①取る，持つ ②持って［連れて］いく，捕らえる ③乗る ④（時間・労力を）費やす，必要とする ⑤（ある動作を）する ⑥飲む

⑦耐える，受け入れる **take a picture** 写真を撮る **take care of** ～の面倒を見る，～を管理する **take off**（衣服を）脱ぐ，～を取り除く **take place** 行われる，起こる **take someone away**（人）を連れ出す **take ～ to** … ～を…に連れて行く 名 ①取得 ②捕獲

□ **taken** 動 take（取る）の過去分詞

□ **talk** 動 話す，語る，相談する **talk to someone about** ～のことで（人）に話しかける 名 ①話，おしゃべり ②演説 ③《the －》話題

□ **tattoo** 名 入れ墨

□ **tear** 名 ①涙 ②裂け目 動 裂く，破る，引き離す **tear up** ズタズタに裂く，引きはがす

□ **tell** 動 ①話す，言う，語る ②教える，知らせる，伝える ③わかる，見分ける **tell ～ how to** … ～に…のやり方を教える **tell ～ to** … ～に…するように言う

□ **telling** 動 tell（話す）の現在分詞 形 効果的な，著しい

□ **ten** 名 10（の数字），10人［個］ 形 10の，10人［個］の

□ **tense** 形 緊張した，切迫した，ぴんと張った

□ **tent** 名 テント，天幕

□ **terrible** 形 恐ろしい，ひどい，ものすごい，つらい

□ **than** 接 ～よりも，～以上に **more than** ～以上

□ **thank** 動 感謝する，礼を言う 名《-s》感謝，謝意

□ **that** 形 その，あの 代 ①それ，あれ，その［あの］人［物］ ②《関係代名詞》～である… 接 ～ということ，～なので，～だから 副 そんなに，それほど **That is all for now.** 今のところ以上です。 **even that** それすら **now that** 今や～だから，～からには **see that**（～するように）気を付ける **so that** ～するために，それで，～できるように **so ～ that** … 非常に～なので…

□ **the** 冠 ①その，あの ②《形容詞の前で》～な人々 副《－＋比較級，－＋比較級》～すればするほど…

□ **their** 代 彼（女）らの，それらの

□ **them** 代 彼（女）らを［に］，それらを［に］

□ **then** 副 その時（に・は），それから，次に **just then** そのとたんに 名 その時 形 その当時の

□ **there** 副 ①そこに［で・の］，そこへ，あそこへ ②《－ is［are］～》～がある［いる］ 名 そこ

□ **these** 代 これら，これ 形 これらの，この

□ **they** 代 ①彼（女）らは［が］，それらは［が］ ②（一般の）人々は［が］

□ **thin** 形 薄い，細い，やせた，まばらな 副 薄く 動 薄く［細く］なる，薄くする

□ **thing** 名 ①物，事 ②《-s》事情，事柄 ③《one's -s》持ち物，身の回り品 ④人，やつ **first thing** 真っ先に

□ **think** 動 思う，考える **think of** ～のことを考える，～を思いつく，～の心当たりがある

□ **third** 名 第3（の人［物］） 形 第3の，3番の

□ **thirty** 名30(の数字), 30人[個] 形30の, 30人[個]の

□ **this** 形①この, こちらの, これを ②今の, 現在の 代①これ, この人[物] ②今, ここ **at this** これを見て, そこで(すぐに) **at this point** 現在のところ, この時点では **in this way** このようにして, このような点で **like this** このような, こんなふうに

□ **those** 形それらの, あれらの 代それら[あれら]の人[物]

□ **though** 接①～にもかかわらず, ～だが ②たとえ～でも **as though** あたかも～のように, まるで～みたいに **even though** ～であるけれども, ～にもかかわらず 副しかし

□ **thought** 動think(思う)の過去, 過去分詞 名考え, 意見

□ **thousand** 名①1000(の数字), 1000人[個] ②《－s》何千, 多数 形①1000の, 1000人[個]の ②多数の **thousands of** 何千という

□ **three** 名3(の数字), 3人[個] 形3の, 3人[個]の

□ **threw** 動throw(投げる)の過去

□ **through** 前～を通して, ～中を[に], ～中 副①通して ②終わりまで, まったく, すっかり **come through** 通り抜ける **pass through** ～を通る, 貫通する **push through** (人ごみなどを)かき分ける **walk through the dangers** 危険を乗り越える

□ **throw** 熟**throw aside** わきに投げ捨てる **throw oneself down on** ～に身を投げ出す, 寝転がる

□ **thrown** 動throw(投げる)の過去分詞

□ **Thursday** 名木曜日

□ **ticket** 名切符, 乗車[入場]券, チケット 動①札をつける ②交通違反の切符を切る

□ **tie** 動結ぶ, 束縛する 名①結び(目) ②ネクタイ ③《-s》縁, きずな

□ **tightly** 副きつく, しっかり, 堅く

□ **time** 名①時, 時間, 歳月 ②時期 ③期間 ④時代 ⑤回, 倍 **from time to time** ときどき **in time for** ～間に合うように 動時刻を決める, 時間を計る

□ **to** 前①《方向・変化》～へ, ～に, ～の方へ ②《程度・時間》～まで ③《適合・付加・所属》～に ④《－＋動詞の原形》～するために[の], ～する, ～すること

□ **today** 名今日 副今日(で)は

□ **told** 動tell(話す)の過去, 過去分詞

□ **tomorrow** 名明日 副明日は

□ **tonight** 名今夜, 今晩 副今夜は

□ **too** 副①～も(また) ②あまりに～すぎる, とても～ **too ～ to** ……するには～すぎる

□ **took** 動take(取る)の過去

□ **toothbrush** 名歯ブラシ

□ **torn** 動tear(裂く)の過去分詞

□ **touch** 動①触れる, さわる, ～を触れさせる ②接触する ③感動させる 名①接触, 手ざわり ②手法

□ **toward** 前①《運動の方向・位置》～の方へ, ～に向かって ②《目的》～のために

☐ **train** 名 ①列車, 電車 ②(～の)列, 連続 動 訓練する, 仕立てる

☐ **travel** 動 ①旅行する ②進む, 移動する[させる], 伝わる 名 旅行, 運行

☐ **treat** 動 ①扱う ②治療する ③おごる 名 ①おごり, もてなし, ごちそう ②楽しみ

☐ **trick** 名 ①策略 ②いたずら, 冗談 ③手品, 錯覚 動 だます

☐ **tried** 動 try(試みる)の過去, 過去分詞 形 試験済みの, 信頼できる

☐ **trouble** 名 ①困難, 迷惑 ②心配, 苦労 ③もめごと 動 ①悩ます, 心配させる ②迷惑をかける

☐ **troublemaker** 名 ごたごたを起こす人

☐ **trousers** 名 ズボン

☐ **true** 形 ①本当の, 本物の, 真の ②誠実な, 確かな 副 本当に, 心から

☐ **try** 動 ①やってみる, 試みる ②努力する, 努める 名 試み, 試し

☐ **trying** 動 try(やってみる)の現在分詞 形 つらい, 苦しい, しゃくにさわる

☐ **tunnel** 名 トンネル 動 トンネルを掘る

☐ **turn** 動 ①ひっくり返す, 回転する[させる], 曲がる, 曲げる, 向かう, 向ける ②(～に)なる, (～に)変える **turn back** 元に戻る **turn into** ～に変わる **turn red** 赤くなる **turn to** ～の方を向く, ～に頼る, ～に変わる 名 ①回転, 曲がり ②順番 ③変化, 転換

☐ **twenty** 名 20(の数字), 20人[個] 形 20の, 20人[個]の

☐ **twice** 副 2倍, 2度, 2回

☐ **two** 名 2(の数字), 2人[個] 形 2の, 2人[個]の

U

☐ **underground** 形 ①地下の[にある] ②地下組織の ③前衛的な 名 ①地下鉄, 地下(道) ②地下組織 ③前衛運動

☐ **understand** 動 理解する, わかる, ～を聞いて知っている

☐ **unhappy** 形 不運な, 不幸な

☐ **unique** 形 唯一の, ユニークな, 独自の

☐ **until** 前 ～まで(ずっと) 接 ～の時まで, ～するまで

☐ **unusual** 形 普通でない, 珍しい, 見[聞き]慣れない

☐ **unusually** 形 異常に, 珍しく

☐ **up** 副 ①上へ, 上がって, 北へ ②立って, 近づいて ③向上して, 増して **walk up and down** 行ったり来たりする 前 ①～の上(の方)へ, 高い方へ ②(道)に沿って 形 上向きの, 上りの 名 上昇, 向上, 値上がり

☐ **upcoming** 形 やがて来る, 来たる

☐ **upstairs** 副 2階へ[に], 階上へ 形 2階の, 階上の 名 2階, 階上

☐ **us** 代 私たちを[に] **let us** どうか私たちに～させてください 略《US》アメリカ合衆国(=U.S./the United States)

☐ **use** 動 ①使う, 用いる ②費やす

名 使用, 用途

□ **used** 動 ①use(使う)の過去, 過去分詞 ②《－to》よく～したものだ, 以前は～であった 形 ①慣れている, 《get [become] － to》～に慣れてくる ②使われた, 中古の

□ **useful** 形 役に立つ, 有効な, 有益な

□ **usual** 形 通常の, いつもの, 平常の, 普通の **as usual** いつものように, 相変わらず

□ **usually** 副 普通, いつも(は)

V

□ **veil** 名 ベール, 覆い隠す物

□ **very** 副 とても, 非常に, まったく 形 本当の, きわめて, まさしくその

□ **Vincent Spaulding** ヴィンセント・スポールディング《人名》

□ **violence** 名 ①暴力, 乱暴 ②激しさ

□ **visit** 動 訪問する 名 訪問

□ **visitor** 名 訪問客

W

□ **wait** 動 ①待つ, 《－for ～》～を待つ ②延ばす, 延ばせる, 遅らせる ③《－on [upon] ～》～に仕える, 給仕をする

□ **waiting** 動 wait(待つ)の現在分詞 名 待機, 給仕すること 形 待っている, 仕えている

□ **wake** 動 ①目がさめる, 起きる, 起こす ②奮起する **wake up** 起きる, 目を覚ます

□ **walk** 動 歩く, 歩かせる, 散歩する **walk around** 歩き回る, ぶらぶら歩く **walk over** ～の方に歩いていく **walk through the dangers** 危険を乗り越える **walk to** ～まで歩いて行く **walk up** 歩み寄る, 歩いて上る **walk up and down** 行ったり来たりする 名 歩くこと, 散歩

□ **walking** 動 walk(歩く)の現在分詞 名 歩行, 歩くこと 形 徒歩の, 歩行用の

□ **wall** 名 ①壁, 塀 ②障壁 動 壁[塀]で囲む, ふさぐ

□ **want** 動 ほしい, 望む, ～したい, ～してほしい 名 欠乏, 不足

□ **was** 動 《beの第1・第3人称単数現在am, isの過去》～であった, (～に)いた[あった]

□ **waste** 動 浪費する, 消耗する

□ **watch** 動 ①じっと見る, 見物する ②注意[用心]する, 監視する 名 ①警戒, 見張り ②腕時計

□ **Waterloo** 名 ウォータールー《ロンドンの地名》

□ **Watson** 名 ワトソン《人名》

□ **wave** 名 ①波 ②(手などを)振ること 動 ①揺れる, 揺らす, 波立つ ②(手などを振って)合図する

□ **way** 名 ①道, 通り道 ②方向, 距離 ③方法, 手段 ④習慣 **get ～ out of the way** ～を追い出す, どかす **in the same way** 同様に **in this way** このようにして, このような点で **on the way** 途中で **way of escape** 逃げ道

□ **we** 代 私たちは[が]

□ **wear** 動 ①着る, 着ている, 身に

つける ②疲れる，消耗する，すり切れる 名 ①着用 ②衣類

□ **wedding** 動 wed（結婚させる）の現在分詞 名 結婚式，婚礼

□ **week** 名 週，1週間

□ **well** 副 ①うまく，上手に ②十分に，よく，かなり **as well** 同様に，その上 間 へえ，まあ，ええと 形 健康な，適当な，申し分ない

□ **well-paid** 形〔仕事が〕高賃金［高報酬・高給］の

□ **went** 動 go（行く）の過去

□ **were** 動《beの2人称単数・複数の過去》～であった，（～に）いた［あった］

□ **what** 代 ①何が［を・に］ ②《関係代名詞》～するところのもの［こと］ **What about ～?** ～についてあなたはどう思いますか。～はどうですか。 形 ①何の，どんな ②なんと ③～するだけの 副 いかに，どれほど

□ **when** 副 ①いつ ②《関係副詞》～するところの，～するとその時，～するとき 接 ～の時，～するとき 代 いつ

□ **where** 副 ①どこに［で］ ②《関係副詞》～するところの，そしてそこで，～するところ **where to** どこで～すべきか 接 ～なところに［へ］，～するところに［へ］ 代 ①どこ，どの点 ②～するところの

□ **which** 形 ①どちらの，どの，どれでも ②どんな～でも，そしてこの 代 ①どちら，どれ，どの人［物］ ②《関係代名詞》～するところの

□ **while** 接 ①～の間（に），～する間（に） ②一方，～なのに 名 しばらくの間，一定の時

□ **whisper** 動 ささやく，小声で話す 名 ささやき，ひそひそ話，うわさ

□ **whistle** 動（口）笛を吹く 名 ①口笛 ②汽笛

□ **white** 形 ①白い，（顔色などが）青ざめた ②白人の 名 白，白色

□ **who** 代 ①誰が［は］，どの人 ②《関係代名詞》～するところの（人） **anybody who** ～する人はだれでも

□ **whole** 形 全体の，すべての，完全な，満～，丸～ 名《the –》全体，全部

□ **why** 副 ①なぜ，どうして ②《関係副詞》～するところの（理由） 間 ①おや，まあ ②もちろん，なんだって ③ええと

□ **wife** 名 妻，夫人

□ **will** 助 ～だろう，～しよう，する（つもりだ） **Will you ～?** ～してくれませんか。 名 決意，意図

□ **Wilson** 名《Jabez –》ウィルソン《人名》

□ **wind** 動〔物にひもなどを〕巻く，巻き付ける

□ **window** 名 窓，窓ガラス

□ **wisely** 副 賢明に

□ **wish** 動 望む，願う，（～であればよいと）思う **I wish ～** ～だったらよかったのに。 名（心からの）願い

□ **with** 前 ①《同伴・付随・所属》～と一緒に，～を身につけて，～とともに ②《様態》～（の状態）で，～して ③《手段・道具》～で，～を使って

□ **without** 前 ～なしで，～がなく，～しないで

□ **woman** 名 (成人した) 女性, 婦人

□ **wonderful** 形 驚くべき, すばらしい, すてきな

□ **wood** 名 ①《しばしば -s》森, 林 ②木材, まき

□ **wooden** 形 木製の, 木でできた

□ **work** 動 ①働く, 勉強する, 取り組む ②機能 [作用] する, うまくいく 名 ①仕事, 勉強 ②職 ③作品 **day off work**《a –》〔平日に取る〕休日

□ **working** 動 work (働く) の現在分詞 形 働く, 作業の, 実用的な

□ **workman** 名 労働者, 工員, 職人

□ **workmen** 名 workman (労働者) の複数

□ **worry** 動 悩む, 悩ませる, 心配する [させる] **worry about** ～のことを心配する 名 苦労, 心配

□ **would** 助《will の過去》①～するだろう, ～するつもりだ ②～したものだ **would have … if ～** もし～だったとしたら…しただろう **would like to** ～したいと思う

□ **wound** 名 傷 動 ①負傷させる, (感情を) 害する ②wind (巻く) の過去, 過去分詞

□ **writing** 動 write (書く) の現在分詞 名 ①書くこと, 作文, 著述 ②筆跡 ③書き物, 書かれたもの, 文書 **writing paper** 便せん, 筆記 [メモ] 用紙

□ **written** 動 write (書く) の過去分詞 形 文書の, 書かれた

Y

□ **yawn** 名 あくび 動 あくびをする

□ **year** 名 ①年, 1年 ②学年, 年度 ③～歳 **for years** 何年も

□ **yell** 動 大声をあげる, わめく 名 わめき声, 叫び

□ **yellow** 形 黄色の 名 黄色

□ **yes** 副 はい, そうです 名 肯定の言葉 [返事]

□ **you** 代 ①あなた (方) は [が], あなた (方) を [に] ②(一般に) 人は **Can you ～?** ～してくれますか。 **Will you ～?** ～してくれませんか。 **you see** あのね, いいですか

□ **young** 形 若い, 幼い, 青年の

□ **your** 代 あなた (方) の

□ **yourself** 代 あなた自身

ステップラダー・シリーズ
シャーロック・ホームズの冒険「赤毛組合」「まだらの紐」

2021年6月6日　第1刷発行

原著者　コナン・ドイル

発行者　浦　晋亮

発行所　IBCパブリッシング株式会社
〒162-0804 東京都新宿区中里町29番3号 菱秀神楽坂ビル9F
Tel. 03-3513-4511　Fax. 03-3513-4512
www.ibcpub.co.jp

印　刷　株式会社シナノパブリッシングプレス
装　幀　久保頼三郎
イラスト　ながたかず
リライト　ニーナ・ウェグナー
ナレーション　ジャック・マルジ
録音スタジオ　株式会社巧芸創作

ISBN978-4-7946-0662-4